Disenchantment
MEANING AND MORALITY IN THE MEDIA

A TAXONOMY OF CONCEPTS IN COMMUNICATION
by Reed H. Blake and Edwin O. Haroldsen

COMMUNICATIONS AND MEDIA
Constructing a Cross Discipline
by George N. Gordon

ETHICS AND THE PRESS
Readings in Mass Media Morality
Edited by John C. Merrill and Ralph D. Barney

DRAMA IN LIFE
The Uses of Communication in Society
Edited by James F. Combs and Michael W. Mansfield

INTERNATIONAL AND INTERCULTURAL COMMUNICATION
Edited by Heinz-Dietrich Fischer and John C. Merrill

EXISTENTIAL JOURNALISM
by John C. Merrill

THE COMMUNICATIONS REVOLUTION
A History of Mass Media in the United States
by George N. Gordon

COMUNICATION ARTS IN THE ANCIENT WORLD
Edited by Eric A. Havelock and Jackson P. Hershbell

EDITORIAL AND PERSUASIVE WRITING
by Harry W. Stonecipher

ENTERTAINMENT
A Cross-Cultural Examination
Edited by Heinz-Dietrich Fischer and Stefan R. Melnik

COMMUNICATION THEORIES
Origins • Methods • Uses
by Werner J. Severin and James W. Tankard, Jr.

ETHICS, MORALITY AND THE MEDIA
Reflections on American Culture
Edited by Lee Thayer assisted
by Richard L. Johannesen and Hanno Hardt

EROTIC COMMUNICATIONS
Studies in Sex, Sin and Censorship
by George N. Gordon

DISENCHANTMENT
Meaning and Morality in the Media
by John M. Phelan

Humanistic Studies in | H | S | | C | A | the Communications Arts

Disenchantment

MEANING AND MORALITY
IN THE MEDIA

John M. Phelan

COMMUNICATION ARTS BOOKS

HASTINGS HOUSE, PUBLISHERS
New York 10016

Library of Congress Cataloging in Publication Data

Phelan, John M.   Disenchantment.

    (Humanistic studies in the communications arts) (Communication arts books)
    Includes bibliographies and indexes.
    1. Mass media—United States—Moral and religious aspects.   I. Title.
P94.P48   1980   302.2′3   80-11661
ISBN 0-8038-1572-7
ISBN 0-8038-1573-3 pbk.

Published simultaneously in Canada by
Copp Clark Ltd., Toronto
Printed in the United States of America

Contents

Preface

Morality and Meaning

Received opinion about the place of morality in relation to the mass media of communication usually restricts it to two relatively narrow contexts: professional codes and controversial issues.

The National Association of Broadcasters, the Motion Picture Association, the American Newspaper Publishers Association, Sigma Delta Chi (The Society of Professional Journalists), and many other organizations, have professional codes that presumably guide, if not bind, their members to certain standards of conduct and to guidelines that determine what is fit for publication in print, on air, or on screen. Regulatory agencies of government administer involved rules for the varied institutions of communication. The regulation can be direct and immediate, as is the Federal Communications Commission's oversight of broadcasters, or it can be indirect and mediated, as is the derived responsibility of the Federal Drug Administration, the Federal Trade Commission, the Securities and Exchange Commission, and many other agencies, to protect the public from false and misleading information. Both the codes of the voluntary associations and the regulations of the agencies have a well-paid priesthood of interpreters which keeps a constant eye on the source and purpose of these rules and which is ever ready with a slick press release for any troublesome sectors of the public.

The codes and the regulations are equally the result of politics in the less noble sense: they are essentially the codification of complaints and petitions from effective lobbyists. Within this framework of economic *realpolitik,* personal responsibility and moral vision about the meaning of human actions, the heart of any system of realistic ethics, have no standing. Responsibility is always legally assigned, rarely morally assumed. It is narrowly defined as legal liability. Ethics becomes a branch of public relations.

The controversial-issue category of ethical concern is not entirely divorced from the code category, since it is also fundamentally rooted in politics: in this case, in the politics of publicly competing or opposed groups within the communications business or in institutions closely allied with the business. By definition, the controversial issue cannot be resolved because it is essentially a journalistic device for recycling old information by attaching it to some current dramatic event, which makes the "issue" newly "relevant."

Although the order of prominence naturally varies with the season, the following litany of topics are repetitively churned within the media mix with reliable regularity:

> Objectivity in reporting and fairness in broadcasting.
>
> Free press versus fair trial.
>
> The right of individuals, corporations, and governments to secrecy versus the public's right to know.
>
> The purchase of news from privileged witnesses or participants from "exclusive rights" to "checkbook journalism."
>
> Management and ownership control over communications channels to the exclusion of certain messages or messengers.
>
> The effect of portrayed violence and pornography on mass audiences.
>
> The validity of advertising claims and the exploitation of certain basic insecurities as motives for buying marginal products.

Devious practices of news management and media influence peddling on the part of government, business, labor, or any powerful entity.

The right of reporters to protect their sources and their notes (in whatever medium) from non-journalistic use.

The obligation of journalists to reveal information to appropriate authority in order to protect life and property.

Each one of these topics can serve as a focus for a cluster of cognate concerns. They are all important and they deserve serious treatment. In media practice, however, they are always the padding surrounding the slick "in-depth" coverage of some current event and so there is mere repetition without development. Readers and viewers are exposed, for the most part, to information without having the opportunity of absorbing ideas or principles.

If ethics and morality are not involved with principles and ideas, they are nothing but a source for empty formulas that serve to organize laundry lists of complaints from interest groups. In short, the journalistic animus that makes these possible topics for genuine moral concern "relevant" to the "latest developments" isolates them from the broader human context of universal freedom and responsibility. Different as they are, both *Oedipus Rex* and *The Gulag Archipelago* raise moral questions. Newsmagazines and television documentaries often bury them.

In fact, there is a general suspicion that both the codes and the controversial issues that trumpet morality could not be farther from genuine moral concerns of the real world.

Is there not a note of staginess in moral outrage over nudity on camera when we are faced with international terrorism and urban warfare? In the "twilight of capitalism" yet still beneath the shadow of the "global reach" of multinationals, should one draw deep satisfaction from the increasingly adult themes of soap operas? In the face of third world starvation, second world nuclear armament, and catastrophic overextension of credit in our very own first world, should we be alarmed at cartoon pratfalls and animated violence? Rome burns and we fuss with the fiddle.

Nevertheless, it is clear that the media, taken as a total

marketing system of information-cum-entertainment, so exclusively present the total world beyond our immediate personal ken that we virtually live within a "mediaworld" whose factitiously concocted morality is unconsciously shared, and abetted, by the great audience, which used to be known as the public. It is vital that we come to grips with the moral implications of the media system. The inadequacy and inappropriateness of "codes" and "controversial issues" as conceptual tools for this task make the attempt all the more imperative.

Instead of rehearsing the familiar litany of controversial issues that pass for moral awareness in media studies or of exegeting one or more trade association codes, it seems more useful to examine three major contexts wherein communications can be related to the perennial humanistic concerns of history, philosophy, and literature.

The first context is that of *Method*. "Functionalism" has been the dominant and studiously amoral method used to study the media and used by the media themselves as institutions. "Humanists and Hardheads" describes the problem of functionalism and pleads for alternate methods drawn from the humanities. "Out of This World" provides an example of what is proposed: a humanistic analysis of a problem often functionally treated—the "fair" representation of minorities in the media.

The second context is found in the contemporary collusion between *Censorship and Consumerism*. These strange bedfellows meet in the politics of professional media monitoring. Public interest media watchdogs, as they are called, are assessed from the viewpoint of political philosophy in "The Consuming Censor."

Technology is the third focus of moral interest. The philosophy of history sheds light on the likely meaning of the latest generation of communications technologies for outer order and inner sensibility. "Cassettes and Catechisms" outlines the communications version of technological determinism.

J. M. PHELAN

Tarrytown, N.Y.
All Hallows' Eve, 1979

Foreword

In 1927, Sigmund Freud posed a question that may turn out to be the great topical conundrum of the twentieth century. "Since men are so slightly amenable to reasonable arguments, so completely are they ruled by their instinctual wishes," he asked, "why should one want to take away from them a means of satisfying their instincts and replace it by reasonable arguments?"

Why indeed? Neither Freud nor his followers to the present seem to display much faith in the ideals of the Age of Reason that have infused the modern liberal with his thirst to do good by returning mankind to its natural state of primal excellence or by educating it to utopian perfection of one sort or another—either beyond freedom and dignity or wallowing in both of them like pigs in slop. Such efforts may indeed be futile and simply provide credence for the familiar conservative claim that maintaining the *status quo* is preferable to tinkering with social mechanisms in the chance the delicate machine may go haywire and break down as a result.

Some of us *must* tinker, it seems, if only to stop other irresponsible cultural mechanics from rushing madly into wild social experiment, philosophical screwballism and political madness that attempts to legislate behaviors and dispositions beyond their natural limits. We prefer freedoms to choose our own "right" road and lifestyle, even in the face of the knowledge that they may be the wrong ones—and to take all consequences if necessary for our foolhardiness and stubbornness. In this era of diminished choice and technological tyranny, however, such deliberate oppugnancy is becoming increasingly hard to carry off, because our apparent antagonisms to the status quo and the best thinking of our time turn out not to be genuine choices at all. As Phelan points out in this book, we oppose, for instance, the vulgarity of advertising in the mass media only at the gravest of risks, simply because the one thing that any civilized libertarian can be sure of is that the inherent evils of censorship are far worse than the crudities of the men who moil for gold on Madison Avenue.

When we consider in their length and breadth those instruments of mass communication that define so much of our world at present so completely and patently for us, choices open to the nay-sayer now become still fewer. We may easily ask for more and better research to demonstrate whether or not our children are being led to perdition by televised cartoon mice chasing televised cartoon cats, whether pornography corrupts the menopausal male or political television shifts our attention as voters from issues to personalities. But to what end, especially since at least nine-tenths of *all* communications research (so-called) that has been attempted in the past three decades is worthless, phony, fatuous and as maliciously beside their points as Trendex ratings, demographic studies and the kind of polls conducted by CBS and *Time* magazine? (The latter purport to record the nation's pulsebeat, but of course do nothing of the sort.) This kind of mechanization and quantification indeed provides us with issues about which to say our "yeas" or "nays." But they are fake issues, part of a meaningless agenda of items drawn from a carefully stacked deck.

Even worse, by-products of the mass media's "secondary

tribalism," as Phelan calls it, seem even to have redefined whatever "reasonable arguments" are left to us (and that Freud mentions) in deceptive and heinous ways. A sterile educational system, dominated by modules of predigested anthologies of slickly packaged "great issues" and quasi-arguments all "cassetted" (Phelan's term) for quick and easy utilization by the masses has rendered the best of us just about incapable of distinguishing between intellectualism and obscurantism, between logic and semantic legerdemain and—worst of all—between scientific thinking and magic.

The demons and demiurges we used to associate with Marshall McLuhan's tomfoolery remain equally as wraithy when they are blamed on Harold Innis or anybody else. They would have little to do with intellect were they somehow blamed on Socrates, an issue on which I think I might find myself ready to cross swords with Phelan, if necessary. And so might I recoil from the facile assumptions associated with Julian Jaynes' notion of the bicameral brain, when and if they are confused with the genuine scholarship and ratiocination of real intellectuals like Eric Havelock and Walter Ong.

The operational rule here is that no amount of complex discourse of colorful theory is true intellectualism if and when it depends upon echelons of organized spooks, imps and gnomes to do its dirty work and fill great and vacuous dark areas of knowledge and insight that, we are assured, require only a little further research to frighten away all of these temporary spirits. When one thinks about it a bit, recent intense interest in the distinct functions of the hemispheres in our brain is more or less inevitable and is probably just a modern metaphor for the disappearance in the recent past of enormous differences men and women were used to imputing to the geographical hemispheres of the earth itself. As rapid, modern transportation eliminated our perceptions of these differences on our globe, it became necessary (or comfortable) to transfer them to our skulls—left (or north) for this function, and right (or south) hemispheres for that function. The now familiar "old brain" became an analogy for the world's once-dark continents and previously unexplored territories. The mystical part of the bicameral brain that once "spoke in voices" of gods was reconstituted as a delightfully poetic analogy for the kingdom of heaven!

All of this is part of the detritus and fallout from what we like to call the contemporary "knowledge explosion"—but is nothing of the sort. It is simply an inevitable turmoil born of the meeting between excessive know-how, techniques, of half-baked fairy tales and myths and the kind of "probing of issues in depth" encountered on Public Broadcasting in America, cute as a bunny and bright with wide-eyed innocence and excessive energy.

Of course Phelan is "disenchanted"! The aforementioned potentially noble and worthy field of communications research, one of his (and my) central interests, has joined a half-dozen older disciplines at *exactly* their weakest and most arbitrary points: where sociology, psychology and political science are the least scientific and the most arbitrary, and where philosophy is least sublime and most facile. He has also witnessed the tragic diminution of one of mankind's most exalted callings, the clergy, as it turned its back on the human spirit and desperately rushed—entirely unprepared—into social work, cultural uplift and the masscom ethic of smooth contempt both for the corporeal individual and the human soul. He is forced to argue with well-meaning (I assume) defenders of "diversity" in the spread of culture for the millions who do not themselves have the vaguest notion of what diversity *is,* or even why it is particularly desirable or undesirable as an integument of culture. (Nor do they care!) Worse, he must demean his own intellect to defend the ideals and spirit of democracy and freedom against assaults so alarmingly crude—and revoltingly popular—that they not only ring John Donne's funeral bell for all of us and for our transient social order, but they almost crack its once-sturdy iron waist.

I am entirely happy to report that *Disenchantment: Meaning and Morality in the Media* is a most impractical book! *Useful* books usually are. When all is said and done, and one talks about the inherent immorality of many of our civilization's most beloved and cherished institutions, it is unwise to look for a list of "recommendations and suggestions" purporting to solve the present crisis and/or undo such deep cultural damage that is, as the reader will discover, irremedial.

The crisis will pass, whether we do anything about it or not. The main issue before us is the anatomy of our own personal disenchantment and the state and fate of our individual moral sense, of which we are each the sole and lonely custodian—that is, if we have nerve enough to put aside our mass paperbacks for a moment, turn off our radios and televisions and roll today's newspaper into an *ersatz* log for our fireplace. The winter promises to be a cold one, friend, and nothing the wit and wisdom Phelan brings to you in the pages of this book is going to offer you gratuitous warmth.

Phelan "tells it like it is," as the youngsters say, and you will see clearly the rights and wrongs and goods and bads we have cultivated in our many and various gardens during the frenetic generation through which we have just—and barely—survived. His humanistic vision is as sharp or sharper than any writer of whom I can think who today attempts to describe this terrain. Like his motives, his wisdom and erudition both speak for themselves with enviable elegance.

GEORGE N. GORDON
Muhlenberg and Cedar Crest Colleges

Part One

MORALITY AND METHOD

1 – *Humanists and Hardheads*

IT IS A MATTER OF AMERICAN FOLKLORE, as created and transformed by public relations, the AP newswire, and gag writers
for Bob Hope and Johnny Carson, that the swallows come back
to Capistrano every March 19th with the punctuality of an oil
bill. With equal reliability and promotional distortion, public
concern for the allegedly evil effects of mass media content on
the great American audience, from day care centers to nursing
homes, cyclically floods the pages and formats of the mass
media themselves. Like the perennial parallelism of *Time* and
Newsweek covers, it is something we have come to expect. The
peep shows of the teens, the flapper films of the twenties, the
gangster sagas of the thirties, the foreign neo-realism of the
late forties, the plastic sex of the fifties, the drug and liberation
dramas of the sixties, the hyper-realistic blood and gore of the
seventies, with all of their print parallels from dime novels to
Hustler, have unfailingly raised hackles and eyebrows not only
in churches and on campuses, but in the planning and editorial
conference rooms of the accused parties and their colleagues.

There is a big market for editorials, think pieces, and "treatments" (with generous samples of the offensive matter) of obscenity, pornography, and violence portrayed in the media.

We have gone over the same ground so many times that one would think we had learned something by now. What does this concern about the effects of the mass media, particularly of television, the most mass of the media, teach us about ourselves and our tangled relationship with the mass media we devour and are devoured by?

My approach will be not to merely repeat what has been said but to try to locate, intellectually and culturally, the points of view within which the popular concern and the public debate whirl and whirl about, like gnats in fixed beams of light that blind rather than illuminate.

The subject matter of the public concern is *content*.

Do films and television and magazines show pictures and motions of the human body that arouse the sexual appetite in a way that offends the moral tenets of feminism, or Puritanism, or humanism, or Catholicism, or of some other movement, group, or philosophy sufficiently known to the public at large? Do such treatments incite certain kinds of individuals to antisocial and even criminal actions, such as rape or indecent exposure?

Does news coverage of accidents, terrorism, murder, surgery, and death-dealing disasters make us fearful and neurotic about the big bad world? Does it possibly incite in some kinds of people a bloodlust that might lead to murder, lynching, or at least an indifference to human suffering? Does drama about crime and dishonesty glamorize these vices and perhaps even teach some young and not so young people how to succeed at crime and fraud?

Questions of this type are all about content and I call them, collectively, the Content Question. This is given the standard media "controversial issue" treatment with the regularity already noted. The formula for media "controversial issue" utterance runs something like this: some say never; some say always; we say sometimes; whatever is clearly evil we deplore, but we will never be so bold as to cast the first stone at any alleged evil.

New versions of the Content Question are prompted by new TV programs, new popular films, legal cases, and prominent sex crimes. You can catch up on the latest version any week now in *TV Guide, The New York Times, Time,* or on some feature segment of network news. The package changes but the inside remains the same, and I suggest that the discussion rarely advances because the points of view are fixed and they direct the discussion without ever being examined themselves. What does this mean in the concrete?

The Content Question is always framed in terms of *effects.*

Effects are always understood as *measurable things* that are *done to* or *for* the audience.

The now notorious report of President Nixon's Commission on Pornography and Obscenity was an almost unflawed example of this approach, which is called *Functionalism* in scholarly circles. A kind of unresolved forced marriage between the mutually incompatible premises of psychoanalysis and the experimental methods of behaviorism, *Functionalism* is the overwhelmingly reigning approach of all "scientific" market research. Market research, in turn, is the solitary guiding light of broadcast programming practices.

Let me illustrate.

What is the *effect* of television news on people; in other words, what does it *do to* or *for* them? Let us ask them through questionnaires (survey method) and let us test them in the laboratory (experimental method). Our returns and our data indicate that news is used to help alleviate loneliness for shut-ins and people who live alone (a sharply rising category in the U. S. Census); that news distracts people from their own worries; that it provides topics of conversation among the semi-strangers who make contact in elevators, at supermarkets, and at other modern replacements for the communal well or the *agora.* Armed with this *functional* information, television executives then proceed to mold the *format* and, *through the format,* the content of the total news treatment so that it is more smoothly tailored to these functions, the "real" meaning and purpose of news. They do this by introducing dramatic sets, charming and attractive "news teams," and consequently news becomes transformed in content: personal tips on grooming and shopping, reassurance on health worries, conversations with "newsmakers" who are the journalistic equivalent of celebrities. A concern for what news does for and to people changes the meaning of news itself. Whether or not the medium is the message, the function dictates the meaning.

Let us now return to the Commission on Obscenity and Pornography. When a "scientific" basis for the report was sought, the climate of opinion then (and now) urged the adoption of a *functional* approach imitating market research. So concern for the meaning of the prevalence of pornography and the exploitative use of sex to sell products and draw attendance became transformed into the functional question: What does pornography do to or for people? Let us ask them and let us test them.

One oft-repeated test was instrumental measurement of penis rigidity among the inevitable college sophomores watching a hardcore porn film chosen for the occasion. It was discovered that after repeated exposure to the same film, interest, ahem, flagged. This not surprising revelation could lend fuel to D. H. Lawrence's celebrated objection to pornography on the grounds that it jaded and therefore destroyed erotic pleasure. For a functionalist, however, this experimental result could only indicate that the *effect* (measurable thing) was short-lived and in the long run negligible. In his terms, no "real" effect.

Functionalism makes a lot of sense in the land of its original application: selling products and politicians. The ultimate purpose of an advertisement for a product or a plug for a candidate is to get the consumer/voter to do something finite and measurable: pick a box off a shelf in a store or tug a lever down in a voting booth. The less debate, reflection, and true deciding the consumer/voter does and the more automatic his action, the better for the marketers of congressman or soup can. This pure functionalism offended Mr. McGinniss (*The Selling of the President*)* and provided an entertaining script for the producers of

Robert Redford as *The Candidate,* but it should surprise no one.

Functionalism reduces both information and art to products that may have either good or bad immediate concrete effects on people viewed as bundles of responses living in a variety of social structures. Truth, understood as either accurate reporting or authentic portrayal of the human condition for page, stage, or screen, becomes irrelevant.

This may have unpleasant political effects both for those who worry about media corrupting us and for those who worry about vigilante groups or government abridging our freedom of speech. As one who worries about both, I feel there must be public attention and discrimination directed at the fundamental issues and not the peripheral distractions of media as a cultural and political force.

If you are a sales or promotion executive of the broadcasting industry, for example, you can point with pride to the great effectiveness and economy of television as a marketing tool. Functional research backs up claims that television and radio campaigns can sell old products to new markets and new, even bizarre, products (such as spray-can cotton candy) to large major markets. If you are a lobbyist for a media trade association in Washington, you can produce reams of data showing that no *content* of any program has ever really had a bad measurable effect on anyone. Alternatively, research does show that children learn from the media many useful things, from the alphabet (*Sesame Street*) to "tolerance for Indians" (*Fat Albert*).

On the other hand, if you are a member of a consumer group or a minority organization lobbying in Washington, or the state capital, you can make a case that your group objects to a program or a paper as a *product* that has a *harmful* psychological or political *effect.* You can then argue that the government should ban the product-program, as it has restricted cigarette advertising, cyclamates and other harmful substances. The media will pay the price of maintaining that they are pushing only products with *effects,* rather than presenting *ideas* which deserve *protection,* because ideas can be norms for human choices rather than mere stimulants for animal responses.

To return to my starting point, then, let me repeat that concern for the effects of the media on American life is often misdirected because the concern is expressed in *functional terms* only about *content*. The result, after almost half a century, is a stubborn evasion in the public forum of the *meaning* of the media as a *form* of communication and as an *expression* of *cultural values*. Scholars as diverse as Stuart Ewen, George Gerbner, James Carey, and Rose Goldsen are approaching the media from other viewpoints which differ with the functional approach and are criticisms of it. In this context, it is fatuous to fund a vast project to measure erections in the hope of understanding how pornography may be a danger to society. It is naive to give current-events tests to high schoolers based on *Time* in the belief that we thus measure their knowledge of the world, rather than the putative "effectiveness" of information packaging.

The humanities should be yielded primacy of methodological place in fathoming the cultural context and moral influence of the media as formats that shape contents and consciousness. In this area, functional questions are more thickheaded than hardheaded: Did media violence tigger the Son of Sam killer? Does media sex create the national venereal disease epidemic or merely mirror it? Rather we should be concerned with what is happening to our own judgment, our curiosity about our own immediate experience, our sense of potency and responsibility about our own lives, our ability to entertain and instruct one another, and our respect for language as a tool for artistry and truth.

An example may point up the inappropriateness of functionalism to these interpretive, humanistic, and cultural concerns (and that is the kind of concern that should be directed toward media "sex and violence," rather than pharisaic scandal or sanctimonious preachments).

Othello is a work of art, a play, and a drama. It can be produced for stage, for screen, for radio; it can be read as a text. We can ask many questions about *Othello* within the context of the play itself, as a supposed world; we can ask other kinds of questions about *Othello* as a cultural expression of the

Elizabethan period; we can ask still other kinds of questions about specific productions of the play that relate to modern stagecraft, cinema art, even contemporary racial attitudes. Why and how did the handkerchief of Desdemona move Othello to terrible and dark doing? Did Olivier add a minstrel-show note to his interpretation of the Moor? To what purpose? And so on. The functionalist would refuse to speculate on the meaning of the dramatic action within the supposed world because it is not "real." He might send out questionnaires to viewers of a given production to see if they experienced an effect: reduction of tension, escape from worry. He might seek to survey minority groups to see if they were offended. Although hardly invalid concerns in themselves, these questions are far from any understanding of what the play means in itself and might mean for us here and now as an expression of ideas, ideals, values, and hopes. More to the point, any true market research about *Othello* would center on the income and buying habits of the potential audience, to link it with product promotion.

Hamlet, functionally, from the moralistic viewpoint, is a corrupting text for any public performance. It paints the king, the symbol of authority, as evil. The protagonist is a neurasthenic whose actions suggest rather sick attraction for his own mother. There is violence and treachery throughout and an ending of despair. No one under 17 should be admitted without "a parent." The meaning and the expression of cultural ideals and ideas are unimportant. The potential *effects* are antisocial.

Functionalism, then, is off the mark and misses the point of literature and art.

Great literature makes assumptions about its receivers that are flattering: they are presumed curious, eager to get out of themselves, ready for growth, critical, yet open; in short, ready for the truth of life and the truth of the imagination. What does canned laughter reveal about producers' assumptions regarding their audience? What must they think we are like? Are they right? In the light of these considerations, it seems to me that ritual bemoaning of sex and violence on television is distracting. Both *Othello* and *Hamlet* have ample sex and violence. What kind of sex and what kind of violence, in what kinds of contexts, enlarge or benumb the human spirit? Only cultural, humanistic, and critical discrimination can help us answer that, and similar, questions.

Some time ago Thomas Whiteside, writing in *The New Yorker,* described with wit and restraint the development of the MH-1 tomato. The MH-1 can take a beating; in fact, it can withstand an impact of 13+ mph, one that most car bumpers cannot handle without damage. This makes the MH-1 ideal as an object for machine picking, forklift stacking, truck hauling, and supermarket-bin endurance. It tastes something like cardboard. That's agribusiness.

What about those new programs on television? Many of them are ideal for world export. They have been test-marketed for the 18-to-34 age group and they have brilliant tie-ins for automobiles, clothing, toys, dolls, paperback "novelizations," and are suitable for recycling in syndication. Some series borrow characters from already proven shows or films so that promotion is already built in. That's show business.

Formats function like the MH-1 tomato and do the same thing to taste. If people buy the tomato and switch on the new season offerings, we have a question of cultural significance, about the mutually demeaning assumptions producers and consumers, performers and audiences, entertain about one another.

Finally, if both media managers and media users look upon art and information programming as just another series of products suitable for MH-1 criteria, then the First Amendment, as well as Aristotle's *Poetics,* are thoroughly irrelevant to American culture. Dostoevski, in his mad-poet manner, once said that beauty would save the world. Banality, then, might destroy it. And that is the "real" pornography and violence of our time.

———

Selected References in Text:

The Report of the Commission on Obscenity and Pornography. A New York Times Book. New York: Bantam Books, 1970.

Joe McGinniss. *The Selling of the President.* New York: Trident Press, 1968.

A study of messages received by children who viewed an episode of "Fat Albert and the Cosby Kids." New York: Office of Social Research, Dept. of Economics and Research, CBS Broadcast Group, 1974.

2 – Out of This World

I

WHILE THE NATIONAL WORRY ABOUT THE effects of the content of the media has been as persistent as it has been unexamined, there has in recent years been a growing concern about the media of an entirely different nature. This relatively new concern is more complex, more loaded with varied, perhaps contrary, assumptions.

The media are accused of failing to represent the real world, of conveying a false picture. Many Americans, none of them proponents of Soviet Socialist Realism or Maoist Revolutionary Truth, believe that the media must represent the real world in some morally responsible way. Sometimes "morally responsible" translates as "mechanically accurate."

Thus, special interest groups have joined market researchers in subjecting television programming, for instance, to a sort of ghostly census. How many housewives, affable homosexuals, black nuclear physicists, bumbling fathers or criminal Italians are featured on the air is routinely tabulated and compared with known statistics about the real world. It has been found that criminals, detectives, young adults, the affluent, sexy young women, whites, and some other types or categories are "over-represented" in media presentations. This has led to all kinds of trade jokes about Lithuanian accountants and Republican transsexuals as possible subjects for television series, paperback pulps, and showcased films in order to introduce balance. These same statistics have also occasioned much oafish sermonizing about "diversity" and "broadcasting in the public interest."

Although it would be easy to ridicule the excesses of vigilantism induced by this concern for conformity to the so-called "real world," I believe the concern to be a serious symptom of a serious cultural condition. Let me try to explain what I think it all means. But first I must clarify some terms or the argument will be misapprehended.

It is not easy to be precise about the term "media" and its frequent equivalent, "mass media." Some people mean network television news, and only network television news, by the term. Others mean New York newspapers. In still other categories, formats may be primarily intended: all-news radio, *New York/New West* magazine graphics.

When I use the term(s), I will generally be referring to the total system of mass distribution of information and entertainment that is both national and international. The prime exemplars of this system are of course the television networks, both in news and entertainment. But the wire services (which supply film, audiotape, videotape and print to worldwide customers); major newspapers, such as *The New York Times, Washington Post,* or *Los Angeles Times* (which are often "flagships" for much larger information-cum-entertainment conglomerates); the national newsmagazines; major production organizations for film, videotape, recordings; and even *ad hoc* production companies for major films of international distribution—all of these varied entities, are also full-fledged media serving the masses. Publishing houses with sophisticated marketing linkages and multimedia associations are part of this vast system as well.

The system is primarily a marketing one, which has prompted comparison with agribusiness. News, plays, stories, jokes, stars, issues, books are like so many hides of beef or cartons of fruit and vegetables which must be freeze-dried, or dehydrated, or compacted, or in some other way packaged so they may move more efficiently to supermarket, drugstore, television set, local theater, or delicatessen. Huge production centers with high technology devices and skilled technicians who are neither farmers nor artists effect great economies of scale. The system is centralized, rationalized, and efficient. The multitude of magazines, radio stations, newspapers, and other media that are hailed as irrefutable evidence of diversity are most often merely retail outlets for relatively invariant wholesale goods. The mellow sound of your friendly Ohio valley station may well have been taped somewhere in Burbank; the local media minister on your television station's routine conscience program may well be discussing an issue brought to prominence by *Time* or *60 Minutes*.

Local editors or station managers have become more like department store buyers, who select, but do not create or modify, already slickly finished wholesale goods. To imagine otherwise is to think a Baskin Robbins store is more diverse than a French restaurant because it has thirty-onederful flavors, whereas all you can get in the restaurant is "French food."

Although the medium may not be the message, marketing does mold formats. Formats, in turn, have a controlling influence on the content of all mass-mediated goods, from frankfurters to *Reader's Digest*.

"Mass media," "media," will accordingly mean some or all of the parts of this system that favors certain kinds of information and certain styles of entertainment. Television is the prime exemplar of the system, but it is only prime, not solitary. In the argument we will be pursuing, narrative formats are the central focus.

In this context, then, how are we to understand a mindset that takes vast blocks of media content and somehow postulates them as forming a monolithic counter-universe which must faithfully, give or take a few bank guards, reproduce the statistics of the "real world"? How are we to relate this concern to the tradition of censorship and fear of art and humor as subversive of good order? Plato feared poetry as a seducer of the spirit through unreal imitations;[1]* Puritans banished much song and imagery as distractions from sober wakefulness in a life of duty. Today some see the media as purveying dangerous stereotypes and alluring deceits which may give people the "wrong idea" about some cherished beliefs or provoke "antisocial behavior." Are these critics merely the latest version of repression and Puritanism?

Although these questions are in part political and social, the social sciences are of little help here, and survey research is part of the problem itself. It is more helpful to locate the mass-media/real-world question within the perennial humanistic preoccupation with the art/life question.

In his delightful essay, "On Fairy Stories," J. R. R. Tolkien makes a distinction between primary and secondary worlds which we may borrow and adapt for our purposes. The primary world is the world of first-hand experience. Our morning cup of coffee and the news we hear on the radio at breakfast are both of the primary world. Secondary worlds do not belong to this plane of existence; they are subcreations ficted by writers: Prospero's island, Alice's Wonderland, Frodo's Middle Earth. So, too, are the lands of the Amazons and the Gorgons, the great bird Roc, and the cave of Merlin. The London of Sherlock Holmes and the Los Angeles of Philip Marlowe, although on modern maps, share the artful isolation and sealed integrity of countries of the mind. The Troy of Hector and the Jerusalem of David, though they testify to the spade as real earth, are also subcreations; in this instance, of nameless chroniclers.

Although secondary worlds are many, and richly varied, they are all in contrast to what Tolkien, within the scope of his essay, envisaged as a single, seamless whole—the primary

* Reference notes are at the end of this chapter.

world. This same world of experience for Peter Berger and other "sociologists of knowledge" is far from a unitary whole. It is fragmented into a "plurality of self-worlds."[2]

The worlds of work, school, family, commuting, clubs, churches may exist on the same plane, but they are separate modules of experience, uncoordinated except by clock or calendar, devices of impersonal number. Modern men and women read on trains among strangers, or listen to the radio alone in their cars between buildings and sets of people who never meet. There is no one module, or world, in which they feel totally at home. Modern people are alienated; they have what Berger calls "homeless minds." Each separate fragment of the primary world evokes a separate self, responding to separate sets of perceptions, expectations, values, and norms of conduct.

A primary world that is whole and entire may have given minds a true home, but it does not follow that its denizens were happy and whole selves. There may be nostalgia for the medieval manor, perhaps even for the Shaker farm, but there remains a loathing for the ant colonies of China and an embarrassed unease in the face of the often forced cheerfulness of kibbutzim. A seamless and escape-proof primary world is suffocating. The secondary world of Siegfried was particularly welcome in dark winter-locked halls.

The "perilous realm" of Faërie, the Garden of Eden and the heavenly city of Jerusalem may at times be grandly transcendent, but they are also humbly escapist. Their utter otherness and distance are themselves enchanting. Until recently this had been a central appeal of all narrative art.

Secondary worlds served the primary world that made them necessary.

For centuries, stories told in words and dance, in music and picture, even in sculpture and architecture, have been of the strange and extraordinary: of gods and heroes and faraway lands, of demons and devils and long-buried times. The ceremonies that mark the great-lived moments of this immediate life—birth, marriage, attainment of majority, death—have long been linked with stories of the distant and tales of the past. The challenges and crises of life—loss of love, conquest, survival of honor, rivalry, treachery, nurture of talent—are intertwined with the dramas of people who never lived and of creatures who could never be people: Odysseus and Siegfried, Helen and Isolde, Satan and Beowolf, Samson and Caliban. These figures transfuse into common existence the bright blood of fable and myth, of enduring art.

Long before people played psychological games, adopted social roles, or chose life-styles (to cite current jargon), boys and girls and women and men dramatized themselves, their troubles, and their triumphs according to basic scripts thrilled to in nursery, learned in classroom, read in libraries or on trains, heard around campfires. Their least eventful moments, as it were, schooled them to live through their best and worst times. For them, life is not a tale told by an idiot but a series of shaped episodes vivified by the ghostly lives of the legendary and the fictional.

Meaning is thus cast on life by varied cues from myth and fable and fiction and chronicle. Old cultures, rich in narratives that have formed lives over centuries, surround the routines of their participants with purpose; their triumphs are more exhilarating, their defeats less desolate. Entebbe rings with the sound of Maccabees.

The coming of modernism was a shattering of the primary world into myriad fragments, from culture to subcultures, without a sustaining, overarching morality or tradition to bind lives into any one compelling pattern of belief or meaning. Complementing this breakup of the primary world there seems to have been a vast and slow shifting of narrative forms and contents to nourish the human heart. Gradually, but quite perceptibly, narrative became more and more "realistic," turning from subcreation to everyday life. The new form, the novel, however artificial in sentiment or improbable in event, dealt with this primary world and with ordinary people. Both Tom Jones and James Bond are improbable, but they are not extraordinary in the way that Parsifal and Orpheus or Hamlet and Jason are.

It is not as if there were no more secondary worlds or

subcreations available, or as if they were now insignificant. The works of Tolkien are long-term best sellers, as are the fables and fairy tales of his colleague, C. S. Lewis. The tales of Richard Adams at one extreme and of Arthur C. Clarke, at another, may well be classed as true secondary worlds. But the overwhelming preponderance of contemporary narrative tales is of the primary world; they even drag apparent subcreations back into the primary world, as does John Fowles in *The Magus* and John Steinbeck in *The Acts of King Arthur and His Noble Knights*.[3]

Fittingly, modern narrative deals most successfully with proper fragments of the primary world, the "inside worlds" of banking, high society, government, diplomacy, medicine, and law. These inside stories are the subjects, and the appealing subjects, of films and television series as well. Mere altered circumstance, not fate nor miracle, could easily insert the readers and viewers of these tales in the "worlds" they contemplate. In fact, the more realistic, or primary, each detail is, the more the narrative is appreciated, like a *Time* report on the President's bathroom at Camp David.

More seriously intended narratives in the media, with an emphasis on "character," do not violate this modern need for "realism." Although the value given seems to be the "realism" of the characters' problems and limitations, the setting must appear to be absolutely authentic. Real spies want to come in from the cold, successful writers are heartbroken when they lose custody of their children, soldiers vomit when they see severed heads, and Harvard law students get diarrhea before exams. Television, the vastly dominating vehicle for narrative today, will promote certain serious programs because they are about "real people." This translates to the limitations and vulnerabilities of those considered bizarre or offensive by the majority of viewers who do not share the "inside world" of the characters portrayed: homosexual parents, terminally ill politicians, aging sex kittens, lonely gangsters. Their weakness is their claim to reality is their claim to attention. Of course, the appeal of the figures of subcreations, of secondary worlds, was more often their strength, or their destiny; their difference, not their fellowship, with the ordinary.

There is a great shift, you will notice, in the type of gift that narrative art brings to its receivers.

The fabulous tale brought the comfort of a fantastically just and happy ending. The heroic sagas gave pride of tribe and incentive for sacrifice. The religious legend promised transcendence through the ordinary. Narratives were ways *out* of the primary world, the home of the mind, to other realms where something could be imaginatively acquired for courage and comfort in the face of primary experience.

All the gifts from such tales can be summed up as moral clarity from enduring values.

Hesitancy, reserved judgment, ambiguity are modern. They belong to the world of multiple real alternatives, to the plurality of self-worlds, to the fragments of unconfident subcultures.

Bruno Bettelheim, an artist of healing homeless minds in autistic children, feels that fairy tales are indispensably therapeutic for all children.[4] But he has the inescapable modern mania for realism. He feels obliged to apologize for the fantastic nature of fairy tales. Children have irrational fears, he tells us, and therefore need irrational reassurance, implying that the healthy person will outgrow both the need and the cure. Enchantment, for the good doctor, is demonstrably useful. The natural cultural use of these tales, their *meaning,* if you will, must be justified for modern parents, who are accustomed to seek and get quite different benefits from the dominant narratives of novels, films, and television.

Depicting only fragments of the primary world, modern narrative neither promises nor delivers transcendent meaning. It does afford companionship, the universalism of vulnerability, the venting of vicarious rage or lust, however banal in motive or meaning. In modern narrative, one is offered a peek into another room of the enormous modern mansion where there are others, in different clothes, with different jobs, just like oneself in age, or values, or expectations. Everyone can observe a media counterpart, as it were, command an episode. There are no subcreations that give shape and substance to the primary world they serve, presenting ideals or models for inner emulation. Rather, there are representative figures which attract universal attention and thus give meaning to various self-worlds.

No wonder New York Police, in a protest against departmental discipline, have literally hoisted Telly Savalas, the television actor who portrays super-macho Detective Kojak, on their shoulders. Associating with him, the symbol-person who is noticed by millions, makes them *real*. Products are more substantial and trustworthy when "nationally advertised." Packages boast in print that they indeed are really "as seen on TV." It therefore follows that human beings, vocations, political candidates, racial types, even ideas, when presented by the media, are granted recognition that confers not merely status, that shadowy sociological category, but actual meaning. An ignored fragment of the primary world is brought into the light and shown to be equal with other known fragments.

In a complex world of millions of strangers, to be noticed is a kind of reward or achievement in itself. This role of modern narrative, so different from the meaning of the secondary worlds of true subcreations, is also a transformation of the very concept of recognition, which was seen to follow achievement, not constitute it.

For the classic Greeks and Romans, the principal spur for excellence and for moral behavior was the formal acknowledgment and admiration of one's own tribe. The very word "triumph" refers to a tribal military ceremony. The laurel, the panegyric, the accolade, kudos—all of these versions of recognition go back to classic tribal rites, whose most intact descendant is the Olympic games, significantly become the super-media event of the planet.

The classic sensibility saw tribal history as cosmically important and tribal recognition was greater the longer it lasted. Enduring in the memory of one's people was immortality. Poets like Horace boasted that their art was a "monument more permanent than brass."[5] For a modern artist this satisfaction is muted. Sartre, no great lover of his tribe, derives comfort from the endurance of *The Words* in the minds of later generations. But his understanding of science tells him that evolution will ultimately wind down so that mind, and all words, will meet final extinction. This ending in an empty theater casts an absurd light on all human accomplishments.[6]

Early Christians, close to the classic heritage, naturally saw recognition as the spur to sanctity. The all-seeing and eternal eye of God may have been intimidating, but it gave the comfort of meaning. The immortality of individuals and the eternity of the community, the company of saints, cast a great moral clarity on every action of every person. This rather ethereal conviction was later grounded in the practical politics of Christendom, with all the apparatus of canonization, relics, and shrines for tribes and places that sought recognition.

The narratives of the past assumed an assured tribal or religious theater of judgment for each person, however humble. Current stories, on the contrary, exist in a primary world where universal judgment and meaning cannot be taken for granted and from which they are often explicitly banished. The astoundingly numerous instances of genocide from Biafra to Bangladesh to Bavaria make each tribe and each fragment of the primary world seem fragile and impermanent. These obvious traits of our times make us even more anxious for recognition and add a nauseating note of nihilism to the dread of loneliness and abandoned old age that haunts our shattered primary world. Art is long, life is short. But art is not quite long enough to compensate for these profound disquiets.

Here it is opportune to return to the current critique of the media as failing to represent the "real world." As we have remarked, modern narrative is far more *realistic,* in almost every sense of this broad concept, than previous narratives of earlier cultures. And the most popular narratives, in whatever medium, tend to be the most realistic. The criticism seems singularly wrongheaded in this context.

But media critics are not looking for what a literary critic would call realism. The criticism is really a cry of anguish from separate and isolated monads: individuals and groups who see the media as the only common forum bridging the fragments of the primary world. Recognition of their fragment is what they want. In America, where more than 23 per cent of households have but a single occupant, almost all households are wired to the media. It is significant that blacks, a minority without sufficient recognition, view television more heavily than do whites and that this gap in viewing habits increases as levels of education rise equally for both groups.[7] They are also among the most vociferous complainers about lack of television "realism."

Media treatment is recognition is meaning.

The total programming of television, radio, magazines, comics, trade paperbacks and other mass distributors of narrative forms can thus be conceptualized as a sort of counter-universe, a counter-primary world that is somehow not shattered into fragments; a Platonic heaven of terminal significance, where to be a celebrity is to be canonized. Whereas only transcendent fantasy could alleviate the tedium of whole primary worlds, only a somewhat mechanical reproduction of the statistics of the using public can assuage the repressed existential terror of homeless minds.

This postulation of a meaning-dispensing media world also offers a plausible rationale for the claim of greater "realism" and thus value on the part of narratives that portray weakness and failure. These vulnerabilities show the common humanity of the minority group represented by the players and give them a fictive fellowship with the scattered and lonely audience, united by the solitude of their media consumption.

A popular film of the sixties, *In the Heat of the Night*, illustrates the point. A redneck sheriff is forced to work on a murder with a black detective from the north. In the small southern town where the murder takes place, the black is considered a "boy." A sophisticated metropolitan detective, the black is outraged by the racist condescension and unmasked contempt that he encounters. Again and again he demonstrates his superiority of intellect and training to the sheriff, who admires him as though he were a talking dog. But when an ignorant big shot slaps the black for his "insolence," the sheriff sees the fire in the black's eye and his instant return of the slap. This rage opens the eyes of the sheriff: "You're just like us!" (to wit: arrogant, proud, tough). The black detective, Mr. Tibbs, became a series character, whose brains and stamina no doubt flattered and pleased black audiences. But the great recognition for rednecks in the audience was the admission of the sheriff, one of their own, that the black was just as ornery as they were, and just as angry at being patronized by rich folks. For a moment the self-worlds touch.

II

The positive stereotypes of the media thus serve a necessary purpose in one sense, but the lack of that second plane, the creation of a truly alternate world that media realism avoids, and must avoid, perhaps causes greater problems. The dynamic balance of whole primary worlds with the secondary worlds of their literature and art had been strengthening to both the individual and the culture in which he participated. The concocted realisms of the media, on the other hand, may ultimately add to the baffling plurality of self-worlds. Indefinite multiplicity, rather than a transcendent otherness, empty room after empty room, is too much like the real primary world of bureaucracy and mass production.

From Kafka to Kubrick, corridors and doors of indefinite extension and number are symbols of contemporary hell. *Seconds,* a John Frankenheimer film about middle-class and middle-age futility, is a most apt mass-media melodrama about plurality without purpose.

A fortyish banker, pale and flabby among the ticking of clocks, wishes his life had been different. His job and marriage are without meaning. For those like him who feel this way and are rich enough to do something about it, there is an unnamed service performed by a mysterious corporation. He goes to a slaughterhouse surrounded by bloody butchers in white coats and is whisked away to an inner sanctum of multiple rooms that suggest an underground metropolis (*vide* the bad-guy headquarters of any James Bond film), a hospital, a prison. Impersonally but with great skill (extravagant skill), the banker is given a new past, a new body, a new face, a new home, a new occupation, a totally new identity. Some kind of accident has been arranged and the corpse found is believed to be his. Plastic surgery, brutal conditioning exercises, psychiatric counseling, forged diplomas, fake awards, even some provided works-in-progress give the ex-banker the module, and the self-world, of a moderately successful painter. In his new world, however, the clocks still keep ticking. New "friends," who sometimes seem to be playing a part, cannot reach him. He cannot paint. He is unhappy. He wants out again—a new, new life.

The mysterious corporation, to which he had willed all his considerable wealth for his first change, is very hard to contact. Through a number of melodramatic episodes, he gets back to the original "headquarters" where new lives are programmed. He begs for a new chance and is treated coldly, like a spoiled child (which he is) who knows not what he wants nor who he is. He is told he must wait while difficult arrangements are made. He waits a very long time, his days passing in a bizarre routine in this limbo land. Every morning he reports to a seemingly vast office where scores of men, suited-and-tied like him, sit dutifully and vacuously at identical desks. One day he is called out by mysterious attendants. His chance has come; he will be prepared for yet more plastic surgery. As he is being made ready in his hospital-hotel-prison cell, the patriarchal head of the mysterious corporation himself enters, and gives him a fatherly talk about "failure": the banker's failure and the failure of the firm to place him well. As the attendants arrive to wheel him to the operating room, the truth screams through his blanked mind. They are going to kill him. They need a body for some other new customer's "accident." The long wait was for a customer who has his general appearance. Indeed, perhaps all the men who come to this firm connected with a slaughterhouse are soon recycled to make room for others. His last conscious act is an animal scream as a surgical drill is rammed through his skull.

The true terror of this film comes from the force of alle-

gory, which breaks through the melodramatic limitations of the
script. The self as totally defined by the primary world—by sur-
roundings, tools, documents—is meaningless. Not the
surgeon's drill, but the mindless nihilism of the whole procedure creates the horror. There is no recognition of any value in
the banker's life. There is no search for justice or truth; there is
no true protagonist, for there is no moral struggle (*"agon"*), no
one character who bridges various self-worlds. And, like Joseph
Losey's *The Servant* and the now near-mythical *Citizen Kane, Seconds* is a dominantly indoor film: cavernous or stark interiors,
dull echoes incarnating hollowness of spirit.

These seriously intended works, and many others like
them, leagues beyond the average mass-media narrative, offer
no truly alternate world which reflects meaning back on the
primary world. Indeed they stylize and enhance the very fragmentation and meaninglessness of the primary world they
never leave behind. The clarification of the problem of pur-
poseless plurality, brought to fevered focus in *Seconds,* is no
small contribution toward the understanding of our predica-
ment, long a function of literature and art. But there is no
complementary reassurance, no cosmic connection, no structure of meaning offered, long the valued gifts of folk narrative
and mythic art. In our current primary world, what is most
needed is what is least presented in narrative forms.

The apparent unifying reach of the mass media, penetrat-
ing "major markets" of diverse strangers with identical programming and parallel commercial messages, the ritually repetitious nature of television news presentations, and the daily
habit of newspaper perusal have suggested to functionalist sociologists that the media are a form of religion—the American
religion. Certainly the perfect fit that Billy Graham and other
evangelists have with the major features of the system—staged
mega-events and promotional hoopla—would strengthen the
parallel.

The parallel is rather with an organized church, whose
dogmas are vague and whose ability to give true meaning to life
is more a matter of promise than performance. The parallel is
to churchiness without faith. For certainly the media are singu-

lar failures in providing meaning and unity of vision. Although to place such demands on the media is almost comically unreasonable from one point of view, the singular sociological position the media occupy does not make these demands unexpected. As we have seen, some such tacit expectation of meaning is at the heart of serious attacks on the media for not representing the "real world."

More average narrative forms that characterize the vast bulk of media programming illustrate this paradox and this failure more vividly than the superior films discussed earlier. As I have argued elsewhere (Cf. *Mediaworld*), the task of programmers is to guarantee comfortable sameness, a sort of flattering mirror image for viewers of just plain folks like themselves, but with some superficial "marginal differentiation" to avert terminal boredom.[8] Middle-aged lawyers, doctors, detectives, pilots, editors, each aided by brash but lovable young assistants, encounter the same crises, told in the same formulaic way, on a nightly basis. *Mad* magazine and television variety shows mine this deliberate policy of banality for constant parody, but the implications are serious. Modern audiences' ingrained sense of living in a shattered primary world of isolated yet identical self-worlds is exacerbated by this type of programming. Although most critics concede this point for the comic-book level of programming, they would like to stop short before the rare but admittedly well done popular narratives about the vulnerabilities of "real people." Yet that difference is demonstrably only a matter of degree, a matter of technical presentation. *Lifeboat, The Poseidon Adventure, Star Trek, Ice Station Zebra, Ship of Fools,* and *Hogan's Heroes*—to follow one theme through its many media variations—differ only in degree as presentations of the unrelieved primary. All levels of mass-media "realism," whether barracks in *Stalag 17* or staterooms on the *Loveboat,* are dead ends of contemporary nihilism.

We must not, of course, imagine a public clamoring for subcreations of surpassing inspiration. The easy availability of modern narratives to modern literates, wired up and within reach of a drugstore paperback rack, is a large factor in almost reversing the setting and goal for narrative. Instead of a thrilling and deep experience of another world, hard to achieve and rarely afforded, the following of a narrative is merely a form of killing time between other only marginally more satisfying primary experiences. The reading or viewing may be chiefly valued as an instructional opportunity (sexual techniques, putting down mother-in-law, ordering elaborate meals) for fragments of life, for the games people play. In that case, the existing drive for "realism" as presentational detail would be reinforced. If a straightforward instruction manual or self-help book is at hand, it will be preferred to the indirect narrative. The explosive increase in sales of such books and the transformation of so many magazines and news programs into instructional formats for everyday "coping" would suggest this may be the case. In any event, one more reason is evident for process and plurality to edge out meaning and integration.

In contrast, the stories of secondary worlds have a sacramental aura that truly does suggest religious parallels. Many of the Christian churches in their sacramental systems have carried to its most developed level the use of symbolism about distant and transcendent events to transfigure everyday life with meaning and recognition. Human birth is linked to the incarnation and the transformation of the world, to spiritual rebirth, when an ordinary man pours water over the body of an ordinary infant. The Eucharist cosmically connects meals and fellowship with immortality and recognition of justice and sacrifice. Sacraments are believed to confer grace, holiness, meaning, on ordinary acts. Such beliefs might be considered charming examples of peasant simplicity; perhaps sacramentalized Christians (or pagan ritualists) might be envied their allegedly easy certainties. However that may be, the "realism" of the media, of the primary-world narrative, has produced a kind of anti-sacramentalism.

By not presenting a type of person, by ignoring an issue or a cause, the media seem to rob them of reality and meaning for a large number of Americans. Conversely, by presenting a "realistic" story about a minority or an "issue," the media merely show that one more fragment exists, along with many others, without order, without purpose. It is recognition without meaning.

This dialectic between pluralism and monism, between monolithic cultures and subcreations, between the fragmented modern primary world and the episodic realisms of its media, is bursting with paradox.

The seamless primary worlds of the past were integral only because they were isolated from other cultures. Since there was no real commerce nor contact with alien cultures for the common man, he could invest his imagination with extravagant tales of totally other "worlds." Today the planet is enveloped in a teeming cloud of electromagnetic signals, laced with cables and optical pipes, pulsing with lasers; borders and barriers are down and the planet itself, the spaceship earth, can at last be imagined in the solitary space it really tumbles through. No wonder we hope we are not alone. Yet all the variety of cultures must somehow be reduced to the familiar so that we can be at home on this increasingly inhospitable sea of rapid technical change.

In this planetary riot of the mind, the media system is seen not merely as a marketing organizer of signals for sale, but as the invisible government of a "global village" unifying a "planetary public" into a common consciousness. It is only natural, one must suppose, that both intellectuals and the ethnically isolated would seek from this technical rationality a metaphysical platform for universal recognition and cosmic significance: not so much a global village but a planetary cathedral, with a prominent place for the pulpit and a democratic list of speakers in place of a priesthood.

Yet the essence of the media system is mercantile. Saviors who seek to capture the system as a vehicle for some unitary "truth" soon find themselves meeting the system's need for turnover. Celebrity is both competitive and, in any institutional sense, short-lived.

The media then, to return to our starting point, *do reflect* the "real world." They just do not explain it, nor do they serve it. Critics who fault the media for not representing the real world have a valid and deep grievance. But the grievance is with the real world, as we have come to know its disturbing diversity since modernization, as much as with its dazzling and distorting media mirror.

————

Selected References in Chapter 2

[1] Plato. *The Republic.* 2nd edition, revised. Translated with an introduction by Desmond Lee. New York: Penguin Books, 1974. Cf. Stephanus 377 ff.

[2] Peter Berger, Brigitte Berger, Hansfried Kellner. *The Homeless Mind: Modernization and Consciousness.* New York: Random House, 1973.

[3] J. R. R. Tolkien. *Tree and Leaf.* Boston: Houghton Mifflin, 1965. ("On Fairy Stories" is the first half of this book.) *The Adventures of Tom Bombadil, and Other Verses from the Red Book; The Fellowship of the Ring; The Hobbit.* Boston: Houghton Mifflin, 1963, 1966.

Clive Staples Lewis. *The Great Divorce; Out of the Silent Planet; Perelandra; That Hideous Strength.* New York: Macmillan, 1946, 1949, 1947, 1946. *Till We Have Faces.* Grand Rapids, Mich.: W. B. Eerdmans, 1964. *The Dark Tower & Other Stories.* New York: Harcourt Brace Jovanovich, 1977.

Richard Adams. *Watership Down.* New York: Macmillan, 1974. *Shardik.* New York: Simon and Schuster, 1975.

Arthur C. Clarke. *Childhood's End.* New York: Harcourt, Brace & World, 1953. *Rendezvous with Rama.* New York: Harcourt Brace Jovanovich, 1973. (among many others)

John Fowles. *The Magus.* A Revised Version. Boston: Little, Brown and Company, 1978.

John Steinbeck. *The Acts of King Arthur and His Noble Knights.* Edited by Chase Horton. New York: Farrar, Straus and Giroux, 1976.

[4] Bruno Bettelheim. *The Uses of Enchantment: The Meaning and Importance of Fairy Tales.* New York: Alfred A. Knopf, 1976.

[5] Horace. *Odes: Book Three,* XXX.

[6] Jean-Paul Sartre. *The Words.* Translated by Bernard Frechtman. New York: G. Braziller, 1964.

[7] Leo Bogart. "Negro and White Media Exposure: New Evidence," *Journalism Quarterly*, Spring, 1972. Pp. 15–21.

[8] John M. Phelan. *Mediaworld: Programming the Public.* A Continuum Book. New York: Seabury Press, 1977.

Part Two

THE CONSUMING CENSOR

3 – Broadcasting and
the American Character

UNLIKE SO MANY NATIONS OF THE WORLD, the United States does not have a ministry of culture. Although one of the most governed peoples on earth, Americans do not formally entrust their heritage to any one bureaucracy. This may be because America is a vast land of disparate regions, peopled by legions of different immigrant tribes. We are left with scattered national repositories of culture, from the Smithsonian and the National Galleries to the Metropolitan Museum of Art, at one extreme, all the way to the National Park Service interpretation centers and preserved pueblos of the southwest.

Far from establishing a unifying state religion, so characteristic of the European nations and essential to the ancient city-states of the Mediterranean, the newly formed United States of America made it a matter of principle and law never to establish any state religion. Despite a heritage of cultural Christianity and a teeming abundance of virtually every creed and code the planet has to offer, there is no one national focus for ethical and moral concerns beyond the prosaic and dusty provisions of the law.

The ancient Athenians had their state theater; the contemporary British retain their crown ceremonials. In our post-Vietnam, post-Watergate period of ethical and cultural stress, it has often been remarked that Americans are at a political disadvantage in not having an official head of state, steeped in traditional authority, separate from the incumbent head of government, so that one could repudiate administration policies without seeming to repudiate the country. The presidency, so often the personification of hopes and fears far beyond its capacity to embody or absorb, has broken its incumbents as often as it has disappointed its devotees. Particularly with Gerald Ford and Jimmy Carter, there has been a consciousness of vacuum at the top.

In the face of our immigrant pluralism and republican origins, there is a craving in America for a moral and cultural focus.

One entity in America seems to meet this need in part without offending our principles. It is broadcasting.

Broadcasting is a national system and broadcasting is a local station. It is a creation of Yankee know-how from the past and a harbinger of futuristic technology. It bestows planetary fame by paradoxically bringing figures down to less-than-life size on domestic screens. The business of broadcasting is a cauldron of competition while its content serves as the ultimate vehicle for glamor; it is the stage for national mourning for a dead president or a platform for national exultation over moonlanded astronauts. Broadcasting seems to be the closest we can come to that combination of cultural, artistic, and moral concerns that has marked every great national heritage from Athens to London.

It is hardly surprising, then, that American broadcasting, particularly television broadcasting, serves as the main arena for religious zeal, moral outrage, state propaganda, and corporate manipulation. Fear of crime becomes immediately welded to fear of violence portrayed on television. Censure of sexual immorality in real life pales before indignation at playacted televised sex. Price gouging and crooked deals are less castigated than are misleading broadcast commercials.

Together with the National Endowments, the closest thing we have to a ministry of culture is the Corporation for Public Broadcasting and the Public Broadcasting System. We do not have an established religion, but we do have a body of doctrines and moral goals embodied in the Communication Act of 1934 (currently the focus of various reforming forces) and court decisions expanding and applying the force of the Act and its agent, the Federal Communications Commission. Advertising, the lifeblood of the current system of broadcasting, is also subject to federal regulation from the Federal Trade Commission.

Broadcasting, then, provides a unique focus for the reforming zeal and righteous religiosity characteristic of America, from the noble experiment of Prohibition to the evangelism of born-again Christians. Today, it is also the focus of the civil fervor found in so many non-sectarian societies founded for moral objectives, from the American Civil Liberties Union to the PTA.

As of this writing there are well over 500 organized groups concerned with the moral obligations of the broadcast industry and the moral tone of broadcast programming. The vast majority are special interest groups dedicated to ensuring that their constituents are fairly represented on the media and/or equally hired by the media. Examples of this type would be the Chinese for Affirmative Action, the National Black Media Coalition, the National Latino Media Coalition. Modeled on the stance and organization of these minority groups, the National Organization for Women Media Task Force and the Gray Panthers Media Watch are subsidiaries of parent groups with broader mandates.

Although far less than 500, there are a score or more of groups, some affiliated with churches or other larger organizations, whose interest in the media is not confined to its service of a special interest. Their concern is moral and ethical. The Media Committee of the American Civil Liberties Union, for instance, is primarily concerned with the safeguard of individual rights and a public atmosphere conducive to democracy. Accordingly, the Committee focus is on diversity, on programming about important issues, and on individual rights (to privacy or to a fair trial, for instance) that may be infringed upon by the media.

The Office of Communication of the United Church of Christ has a very broad range of concerns, but is best known for its advocacy of local community rights to adequate access and coverage by all locally based media. The United Church Communications Office (UCC), in fact, was the instrumental lobby in accomplishing the first denial of a station license for failure to meet local community needs (*UCC vs. FCC*, 425 F2d 556—D.C. Circuit 1969) and in another case set the precedent by which all other broadcast groups have acquired legal standing: Since 1966, the FCC has been obliged to hear the complaints and petitions of bona fide groups concerned with the moral obligations and quality of broadcasting (*UCC vs. FCC*, 359 F2d 994, 1005—D.C. Circuit, 1966).

Action for Children's Television (ACT) is another broadly based group that seeks to improve the general quality of programming, notably with regard to violence and commercials as they affect children and parents. The National Citizens Committee for Broadcasting shares the concerns of UCC and seeks to provide information services for other groups to achieve their goals. All of these groups rely heavily on legal actions before regulatory agencies and the courts to achieve their goals. With their generally low budgets, they must have recourse to public interest law firms (PIL) that provide high-quality, low-cost legal aid. Outstanding among these is the Citizens' Communications Center which handles a large caseload of appellate and administrative issues involving ownership standards, pay cable and subscription television rules, obscenity, access, fairness, renewal (of license) standards, station formats, ascertainment of community needs, station transfers and sales, and many other technical matters with public and moral import. These types of groups and their concerns are centered on *power,* with *who says* what to whom, and are often called "public interest groups." (The Communications Act mandates that stations be licensed in "the public interest, convenience, and necessity.") The National Citizens Committee for Broadcasting has recently affiliated itself with Ralph Nader's coalition of organizations to become a formally designated Public Interest Research Group (PIRG). UCC has recently spearheaded the formation of a Telecommunications Consumers Union to aid local groups with expert advice, information, and action-producing tactics.

These public interest groups are very similar to other organizations, but their fundamental drive is distinctive. The National News Council, for instance, deals more with print than broadcasting (to date) and serves more as a complaint bureau for individuals who have felt cheated or misused by the media in a specific instance. The Council, established by the Twentieth Century Fund in emulation of European press councils, lacks the authority to impose any penalties or to force retractions, unlike its foreign counterparts. There are other groups that are more concerned with *content* than anything else. Such would be the religiously motivated Morality in Media, with its campaign against alleged pornography and drug-abuse advocacy in all media, and Accuracy in Media, with its concern that any criticism of "the American way" or of allies of America be balanced by equal criticism of communist regimes or black racist regimes.

The aforementioned groups, concerned primarily with content, tend to be conservative (unless they are minority special interest groups as well). Still other groups, radically critical of the *structure* of the broadcast industry, tend to be quasi-revolutionary and anti-capitalist. A relatively moderate group of this type was the Network Project, subsequently transformed into the Public Interest Satellite Association, which itself is about to undergo another transformation. These kinds of groups believe that if the structure is radically altered, both control and content will also be changed. If there were movement, for instance, to locally owned stations broadcasting locally produced programming, and thus a move away from AT&T landlines as the principal distributor of television, then the content will be radically altered as well. New technologies may bring this about without any help from radical lobbying.

Our principal focus here is on the public interest group as

a lobbying force that unites the consumer movement with a political notion of the public interest and fires both with a reformist zeal that has at times evangelical enthusiasm and righteousness.

The result is often a peculiar marriage of convenience between consumerism and (no other word will serve) censorship.

4 – *Censorship and Consumerism*

IT IS A CLICHÉ THAT TELEVISION IS AN advertising medium that gathers and arranges troops of potential buyers, according to age, preferences, and income, and sells their attention. Behind the cliché is the real consequence that virtually all American communications media are dominated by the methods and mentality of product promotion. The television commercial, as the most dollar-dense and talent-packed message unit in the system, becomes the style and status model for most other types of messages. Presidents and senators, museums and libraries, hospitals and research institutes, are all displayed to the public in the format and with the animus of product promotion.

Products are promoted primarily by associating their purchase with some desired effect. A brighter smile, not toothpaste, is sold. A glamorous "life-style," not a condominium, is commercially offered. The kind of consumer protection championed by Ralph Nader has ironically been brought about in part by this consciousness of consequences. Naderism forces us to concentrate on real effects with pitiless precision: Cars kill;

chemicals poison. In either case, the product itself is lost and becomes but a glass between the purchaser and his desired result or the consumer and his feared consequence.

It is a small step from seeing a product as in itself fraught with promise or threat to conceptualizing a commercial for a product as the automatic cause of the ultimate result. The commercial becomes the prime mover—sports car commercials featuring speed and dash lead directly to death on the highways. Television, the premier stage for dramatic promotional messages, can itself be conceived within this framework as a sort of mega-product with inevitable social or cultural *effects*. Each program then becomes a specific cause for a specific effect.

This questionable but broadly accepted line of thinking permeated the political climate which commissioned the Surgeon General to launch a series of studies on the *effects* of televised violence. Does it produce real violence beyond the screen?

Despite the difficulties of accurately defining "violence" and the methodological obstacles against pinpointing narrow sources for human motivation, the general trend of the studies and the only mildly qualified conclusions of the official report on these studies was that, yes, the programming of violent material induces violent behavior among the audience and the violent behavior is socially dangerous.

A few years before this report, a similar federal initiative created the President's Commission on Pornography and Obscenity, which authorized extensive survey and experimental research (in format much like the later studies on violence) to see if a link could be established between pornographic films and books and objectionable sexual behavior. Although "pornography" is a much more narrow concept than "violence," there was greater difficulty in defining terms for this study and general reluctance to see a causative link between "art" and "life." In the end, with some dissent among the commissioners and with sporadic if outraged rejections among the public, the Commission felt there was no compelling brief for ascribing any real social ills to alleged pornography or obscenity. It is perhaps arguable that the underlying problem was the impasse over agreeing about what is objectionable when it comes to sex, apart from brutal rape, which already fits the broader "violence" category.

Whether or not one accepts the conclusions of either set of studies, they share a common assumption that programming material is most aptly judged on its alleged *effects*—physical, measurable effects. In a free country one cannot condemn ideas or meanings, so why bother to judge them at all? With the revelation of bizarre mass murders from California to Chicago to Texas, there exists an emotional consensus that violence is threatening our lives and our minds as well. If criminal violence is evil, then anything that causes criminal violence is evil. Therefore, programming content can be judged evil in its probable effects and should be banned.

The desire to control speech because of probable consequences of the speech is the heart of all censorship movements. Comstocks and Cromwells have always looked at human expression as dangerous because of possible political, religious, or sexual results. Intellectuals value ideas because ideas have consequences. Censors fear speech because it has effects.

Censorship is rightly associated with repressive totalitarianism and the tyranny of the majority. In contrast, consumer protection is rightly identified with the rights of individuals in the face of corporate power. Today our obsession with symbols for sale and our functional tunnel vision of *effects and effectiveness* have made it credible to present censorship as consumer protection, while at the same time advertisers can condemn a concern for honesty and truth as censorship. Our heritage does not fit our circumstances.

It was in this moral atmosphere that Action for Children's Television was born. ACT considered the recycled cartoons of Saturday morning, the kidvid ghetto, as facile presentations of objectionable violence and tacit racism. Many of the commercials during this time gave children false hopes for supertoys that did not work so well nor look so solid at home without studio lighting. Other advertisements pushed junk foods and encouraged kids to demand them from harried parents.

ACT began in 1968, growing from a central cell of concerned mothers to eventually include teachers, doctors, psychiatrists, and other professionals as well as thousands and thousands of parents. Mrs. Peggy Charren, the original central mother, was and is the soul of ACT, which she has led with impressive charism. Her promotional talents are shared by Everett Parker of UCC, Philip Jacklin of Committee on Open Media, Thomas Hoving and later Nicholas Johnson of the National Citizens' Committee for Broadcasting and other leader-founders of media-reform movements. Ironically, all these people know how to manipulate journalists to command media coverage. As does Ralph Nader, the archdeacon of effective protest, they know how to create pseudo-events and come up with quotable one-liners. Without this promotional hoopla, dedicated but for the most part invisible genius among public interest lawyers like Earl K. Moore or Al Kramer would go unfulfilled.

Mrs. Charren has been an unusually successful fund raiser and organizer. In 1978 ACT had a budget in excess of $300,000, when barely a half-dozen groups exceeded $100,000 and virtually all others were under $15,000. Many groups with "National" in their title consist of one poorly paid activist, a volunteer secretary, some occasional helpers, a letterhead, a telephone, and frequently an empty office with a phone-answering tape recorder. In this setting Charren's success is all the more remarkable, with over 7,000 members contributing a minimum of $15 annually and with a number of foundation and corporate grants! ACT has paid for its own "effect" research and supports the usual monitoring activities. Following the impressive lead of UCC, ACT has been most active before the regulatory agencies, most notably the FCC. ACT has in turn, it seems, inspired UCC's move toward service for local groups. Remember, broadcasting is always locally licensed, so this is the exposed nerve that can be subjected to legal pressure.

The censorship-consumerism connection is best displayed in ACT's lobbying activities with regulatory agencies.

As early as 1970 ACT filed a petition with the FCC to ban advertising from children's television. The petition was backed up with 100,000 supporting letters, more than any other petition up to that time had ever aroused. As the former campaign director for presidential aspirant Barry Goldwater, then FCC Commissioner Dean Burch had a rueful respect for big numbers. Although four years later the FCC refused to pass such a rule, the acknowledgment of the standing of the petition did pressure the National Association of Broadcasters to advocate officially a reduction in advertising time during children's programming. In 1978 ACT came back with an even stronger petition for the same goal. Between the first and the second petition in this matter, ACT had appeared before a dozen congressional oversight and investigating committees, had filed petitions and amicus briefs (supporting argumentation for the petition of some ally) before the FCC and the Federal Trade Commission (FTC) a score of times, often with success. Between 1970 and 1978, special vitamins for children were no longer advertised, the hosts for children's shows could not advertise personally for products on those same shows; roughly 40 per cent of children's advertising was dropped on weekends. ACT takes much of the credit for these measures.

ACT had become a regular customer of FCC notices of inquiry and rule-making procedures. A notice of inquiry is a formal announcement of deliberations being initiated toward making some specific rule or set of rules for the industry regulated. The notice is intended to attract all interested parties to present positions germane to the proposed rule.

The Communications Act of 1934 (and any likely subsequent revision) carefully restricts the FCC to the role of traffic manager and format regulator, with no authority to deal with content, already generally protected by the First Amendment from government interference. The FCC has steadfastly refused to ban advertising on these grounds and has been mightily encouraged in its refusal by the broadcasting and advertising lobbies. ACT has never been able to *impose,* through governmental power, any reforms of programming that the networks and stations did not voluntarily adopt.

Most resourcefully, ACT realized another approach and

another agency might achieve the controls the FCC was reluctant to enact in the teeth of constitutional objections and self-righteous indignation against alleged censorship.

ACT found the key in the status of advertising.

Legally, advertising is commercial speech. While speech may be free, commerce may be regulated. Commercial speech conjures up the world of contracts, with provisions for full disclosure, penalties for misrepresentation, and sanctions against failing to meet commitments. The Federal Trade Commission (FTC) has long regulated these aspects of advertising, with particular concern for "deception."

The Truth in Lending Act and the Magnuson-Moss Warranty Act, both fruits of the Nader movement, protect adults from fraud, deception, and misleading terms of contract. The media savvy of Charren had long ago led her to present children as one more (or the very ultimate) "minority" which did not receive equal protection from the law. Children were not protected from deceptive advertising with regard to toys and candy. Adults benefited from public service messages on the dangers of smoking before broadcast advertising for smoking was banned utterly. Cigarettes lead to disease. Candy leads to cavities.

Note the march of the logic. Federal agencies regulate the safety of products, from jumbo jets to hair dryers. Federal agencies regulate communications. Federal agencies regulate business contracts and terms of sale in certain instances. Federal agencies test for dangerous effects of substances, such as food additives. Federal initiatives had funded studies to evaluate the consequences of pornography and media violence. If a product can be banned as harmful because of its effects, a commercial can be banned because of *its effects*.

Few have choked on the awkward course of analogies because advertising has long associated speech in the public mind with palpable products of measurable effect.

It is but one more short step to include any message, any act of speech, any presentation of drama or art (the format of so many commercials) as merely a production (a term common to show biz and manufacturing) with effects. Meaning and beauty, learning and sensitivity, knowledge itself, become mere side effects with no "real significance."

In 1978 this logic led to a rule-making proposal, urged on by ACT, that can be seen as the last word in consumer protection and as the first small cloud of state censorship on the American communications horizon. Following standard practice, the Federal Trade Commission issued the following Notice of Inquiry:

A) Ban all televised advertising for any product which is directed to, or seen by, audiences composed of a significant proportion of children who are too young to understand the selling purpose of or otherwise comprehend or evaluate advertising.

B) Ban televised advertising for sugared food products directed to, or seen by, audiences composed of a significant proportion of older children, the consumption of which (*sic*) products poses the most serious dental health risks.

C) Require televised advertising for sugared food products not included in paragraph (B), which is directed to, or seen by, audiences composed of a significant proportion of older children, to be balanced by nutritional and/or health disclosures funded by advertisers.

The Notice then goes on to list four other "remedies" that are less drastic than the proposed rules as alternatives. The alternatives essentially "limit" rather than "ban" and need not distract us at this point. The Notice also lists 14 "general questions and issues of fact" raised by the proposal which the Commission invites the public to comment on. These questions and issues are at the heart of the matter, for they are the sources of most objections and the debating points around which the hearings proved to revolve. Including but transcending the stated questions and issues, our discussion immediately raises the following thicket of puzzles: How uniform is the development of judgment in children of varying ages or of the same age? Does sucrose itself have some balancing good effects on the bodies of growing children? How tight a line can be drawn between advertising for sucrose and any probable bad effects of sucrose? How will the selection of only one medium for the proposed ban affect demand for candy among children? How can the ban be restricted to one harmful substance only? How does one justify restrictions on programming "directed to, *or* seen by" a specific group on a medium that reaches an undifferentiated mass with varied needs and interests?

Not surprisingly, a firestorm of protest erupted immediately from the legal brief and press release machinery of networks, syndicates, program producers, toymakers, candy manufacturers, advertising agencies, and most mediaworld lobbyists. Reliably, "free speech," and "free enterprise" would be effectively invoked before the Commission. Although the arguments of these interested parties are not necessarily wrongheaded nor insincere, their predictable pleading makes them of less interest than the alarming logic of the proposed rule itself and of the supporting brief from ACT penned by Mr. Moore.

Mr. Moore supports a total ban of advertising aimed at very young children and a ban of advertising for sugared products aimed at children of any age. The core of his argument rests on the understanding of "deception" within regulatory law and on professional assessments of the judgmental powers of children.

What is the legal understanding of "deceptive" advertising?

In real estate and stock offerings, and in some other sales situations of complexity and subtlety, a prospectus spelling out all the facets of the matter must be given to the purchaser or investor for his study before any transaction takes place. Although frequently in terms only a trained person can interpret, a prospectus meets the requirement of "full disclosure" of all reasonable consequences of the purchase. To attempt to sell in these circumstances by slogan or sales pitch alone would be to withhold "full disclosure" and therefore would technically be considered "deceptive advertising," which is illegal.

In general, most items for sale do not require formal prospectus because the average adult is presumed to be alert enough to realize the consequences of the purchase. In these matters, the "net impression" of an advertisement must be positively misleading in order to be deceptive in the legal sense. By referring to "net impression," realistic leeway is given advertisers for dramatic exaggeration and other tricks of the trade that men of the world accept as part and parcel of persuasion. Each and every single statement is thus not subjected to a reality test of literal truth. Thus, the FTC does not automatically condemn the common advertising cliché of the comparative absolute—"whiter whites," "98% more pure." We are never expected to ask, "Than what?" The rule of "net impression" gives room for common sense in evaluating the amount of permissible "deception" expected in advertising.

Relying on the testimony of child psychologists and functional testing, as well as on (thank God!) common sense, ACT points out that children do not have the judgment and maturity of adults. Very young children are simply incapable of seeing any undesirable consequences to the purchase and subsequent use of any product that is presented persuasively and attractively. The sincere smiles and honest voices of paid endorsers on television and radio are perceived as belonging to friendly adults who are extending personal advice to their little friends. For very young children always, and for all children sometimes, the "net impression" of any advertisement is in the legal sense "deceptive" because "full disclosure" is impossible.

A notoriously clear case of such deceptive advertising, for ACT, is present in television advertising aimed at children for candy and other sweets for sale. Children are utterly defenseless before the carefully crafted commercials of master persuaders urging them to get candy. Even older children, who have some idea of the selling purpose of commercials in general, do not have the mature discipline to exercise restraint in their appetite for sweets. And it is very clearly established that sucrose causes tooth decay and that tooth decay is particularly endemic among children. Therefore, the proposed FTC ban is called for, and is in keeping with the spirit of existing laws.

Mr. Moore and Mrs. Charren are sensitive to the charge of censorship. Again and again they make it clear that they are interested solely in protecting the consumer rights of a neglected minority—children. Mrs. Charren has made it clear that she would not seek to restrict ads for contraceptives because such restrictions are identified with censorship and violate—in her view—the First Amendment, which she holds as sacred as any journalist does.

Nevertheless, the arguments of Mr. Moore and the rhetoric of Mrs. Charren raise fundamental objections to our entire marketing culture that simply cannot conveniently be confined to the nursery—and perhaps they both know this only too well.

In a speech at the Georgetown Law Center six months before the FTC proposed its new rule, Mrs. Charren stated: "There are some products for which there can be no fair messages."

There are two disturbing assumptions in this assertion.

The first assumption is that some objects are essentially evil or dangerous, independent of human choice and human use. It is the grand-daddy assumption behind all technology-as-devil positions and needs no lengthy refutation here.

The second assumption is that advertising, by and large and for most products, gives out "fair messages," by which I presume is meant honest, unbiased, neutral information. This is the party line of all advertising apologists: advertisers provide vital information in a democratic society where people are entitled to make up their own minds without some national nanny to safeguard their own best interests. To their customers advertisers present the entirely more plausible view that they are wizards of manipulation. This wholly legitimate claim can be made in some disingenuous forms so that advertisers can have their public service image while eating the real cake of their control over consumers. In this rhetoric, marketers will talk of engaging in research to discover the "unconscious needs" of a target in order to tailor advertising to "reveal" these needs to the very possessors, who heretofore lacked that much self-knowledge. This Socratic view of merchandising, if you will, has been used to explain cola drink campaigns in underdeveloped countries.

Advertising is, of course, only incidentally informational. It has no more interest in a "fair message" than an editorial or a sermon. Advertising does not seek to appeal to mature judgment; it seeks to cloud it. People do not buy medicine; they buy relief. To pretend that adult consumers have the opportunity, or even the inclination, to act rationally on informational advertising is to misapprehend the teeming marketplace. To introduce "balance" in this context has the logic of madness. Slick theater skits urging patronage of betting parlors are followed by lightning-like voice-overs cautioning people to bet with their heads not over them. A series of commercials urging installment buying, bank credit cards, immediate vacation travel "before it is too late," and other flames for inflationary fires, is followed by a public service spot lamely exhorting thrift as a patriotic duty.

Neither evangelists nor politicians accept the classic economic model of rational man maximizing his sober satisfactions. Why should advertisers? Advertising appeals, and successfully appeals, to the child in all of us. In this context, it seems a bit silly for ACT to contrast the helpless irrational child with Mr. Clear-thinking Adult Consumer and to concede that he is fair game for procedures that children must be shielded from.

ACT is disturbed that sports stars and other childhood idols are hired endorsers of candy and toys on television commercials. Children do not realize that the endorser is being paid for what he says. Does this imply that therefore he or she is probably lying? If commercial endorsements have this essential flaw, why should adults be exposed to them? Is it because their mature adulthood renders them impervious to seduction by celebrities?

After the dreadful blow-out of its reputation due to thousands of defective tires sold and later recalled, does Firestone believe that having Jimmy Stewart narrate polished dramatizations about the dedication and quality-mindedness of its founder will have little effect on Mr. Rational Consumer? Is it merely coincidence that Mr. Stewart has spent a lifetime being cast in roles of common-man decency and is a stereotype of humble integrity? Would a less-known actor serve as well to convey *information*? Somehow Don Rickles does not seem right for the part, which must convey credibility, not necessarily truth. To judge this practice as "fair" or "unfair" is to miss the point. Whatever is being done, it is not the simple presentation of information to presumably rational adults.

In the long run, every adult is profoundly affected by the constant exploitation of basic insecurities, from fear of sexual failure to fear of bankruptcy, that our promotional culture enlists to provoke impulse buying. If the FTC should ban advertising for very young children, how can it permit hard-sell real estate and insurance commercials beamed at the elderly and the infirm?

Sugar can give children cavities. It can kill adults, some of whom are especially vulnerable to heart attacks, diabetes, high blood pressure and other ailments exacerbated by high caloric intake. Adults are supposed to know all about these dangers. Do they know about the high sugar content of ketchup, cheese spreads, and salad dressings? Do they know that sodium nitrite, when exposed to cooking heat, is often transformed into a proven carcinogen, nitrosamine? Do they know that ham, pastrami, sausages, and many other processed meats contain sodium nitrite? Should meat advertisers pay for nutritional messages and balancing warnings about dangerous food additives? Without this knowledge, adults are as helpless as tots in front of unwrapped Milky Ways.

Over 300 years ago, John Milton argued against the British government's undertaking control of the content of all printed material. Among his arguments was the practical one that it simply did not stamp out the evils it was aimed at while hindering a lot of harmless activity and perhaps even preventing positive benefits to society. He also pointed out that once begun, it is hard to limit. Why not ban Morris dancing? he asked. Milton lost this argument and the censorship of the state lingered on for more than a half-century. If we accept the arguments of ACT's brief, how can we limit the FTC to the tame controls of the proposed rules?

Behind the broad critique and the narrow measures there lurks one of the more enduring dogmas of American folkways. The children's world should be artificially shielded from this shabbiness so that the young can indulge illusions of justice and truth. Let us place all of our concern for honesty and fairness in a tidy little box and deliver it to the nursery and primary school. Let us make the home a shrine of love. But never forget the impracticality of these refuges from the cutthroat marketplace—"the real world."

If this cynical view of the world is correct, then it would seem more practical to expose children to all kinds of fake puffery so that early in life they can learn to recognize it. It is never too early to learn that apparent friends may have ulterior motives. However, if this cynical view is false, if American culture is connected to much that is idealistic, to community spirit and to creativity, then we ought to uproot hucksterism from all of public communications, beginning with government press conferences.

It has been noted that one of the unintended effects of constant propaganda, as in Soviet Russia or Maoist China, for instance, is to make hardened cynics of intended dupes. It is impossible to get them to believe anything, although fear and self-interest may motivate them to do whatever the regime requires. This effect, which we may call the hard-heart factor, is the real danger to children, and to the rest of us, from constant exposure to exaggerated claims, incomplete disclosure, misleading statements, and show biz in place of straightforward dealing. It is the reason so few believe there is a genuine shortage of energy rather than the more credible profit-and-tax crisis for the really big spenders.

That commercials may increase the number of cavities in kindergarten is really rather small beer for the effort that has been mounted. It seems a shame that concern for teeth should move our society against organized deception because a direct appeal to truth is too weak.

5 – Freedom of Expression
and the Public Philosophy

IF TELEVISION COMMERCIALS (which assuredly have no monopoly on mendacity) are to be transformed into vehicles for truth, the national experience with Prohibition, gag laws, and attempts at prior restraint of publication does not argue well for government regulation as either an appropriate or effective agency for this purpose.

Following the precedent set by tobacco merchants, toy and candy manufacturers would sooner abandon the television market than be compelled to finance messages that discourage the use of their products. Network management has indicated that without this financial support they might well abandon programming for children altogether. Although ACT is in favor of more, rather than less, programming for children, it might concede that nothing at all would be better than what is currently offered. Surely it would not be a cultural disaster. Such a chain of events cascading from a government rule to compel "balancing" messages reminds us that control of some messages, even commercial ones, leads to control of more messages.

In our sophisticated applications of market research, much advertising is positioned very carefully for specific audiences, even when the advertiser is technically not the sponsor of the programming that surrounds it. Control of certain types of commercials leads to effective censorship of the type of programming they are associated with. If the FTC were to find that commercials for beer, power tools, and automobiles were inevitably deceptive, then professional football might well leave the home screen. Once again, this might not prove to be a national disaster. Nevertheless, the federal power to censor—for that is what is being proposed—commercials ineluctably grows into the federal power to control the central podium of our society.

As a nation we are thus faced with a serious dilemma.

On the one hand it is evident that much of our public discourse is deceitful and much of our public entertainment is degrading to such a degree that many good people—none of them Puritans or fascists—want to put a stop to this mental and moral pollution. On the other hand, we have a tradition of freedom of expression that is both deep-rooted and delicate. The road toward legally safeguarded individual rights from Magna Carta has been long and arduous. Our own recent history (the Palmer raids of the twenties, the Smith Act of the forties, the McCarthy period, the harassing of Vietnam dissenters in the sixties, among many other unproud episodes) shows that the essential freedom of the noble American experiment has come perilously near termination with the consent of the majority.

How are we to promote decency and honesty without recourse to state censorship or some form of thought police?

The first step toward a solution is a proper fix on the position of the problem. Today, expression is contained in a complex technical vehicle which is generally referred to as the mass media. This circumstance and our heritage clash fundamentally. The conflict can usefully be examined under five rubrics:

- Moral conscience versus technical rationality.
- The public interest versus special interests.
- The public philosophy versus the market model.

• Positive freedom versus negative freedom.
• Cultural controls versus legal restraints.

Moral Conscience versus Technical Rationality

Truth as an ideal and the importance of telling the truth are moral concepts. They are the result of centuries of moral development, of inner growth, spurred on by the reflective awareness of great men like Socrates, St. Paul, St. Augustine, Thomas Aquinas, Kant, Spinoza, Dewey and Freud. These inner convictions are outwardly enshrined in institutions of law that govern contracts, detailed by centuries of commercial experience. These ideas, laws, and customs have been given meaning within religious belief systems and have been given sanctions by ecclesiastical organizations, whose codes and creeds have been ingested by generation after generation with mother's milk. Today, when two individuals talk to one another, when families celebrate a wedding, the aura of these traditions of reliability, trustworthiness, and honesty—of telling the truth and abiding by it—is profoundly present, even when honored in the breach. Morality is personal, because only a person can be held morally responsible for his actions. Persons, in turn, are social and tribal creatures. They act on what they think and feel, and these inner realities are shaped by outer schooling and training. A man's word is his bond and a man's work bears his mark, his signature, his personal warranty.

Large corporate organizations are persons only legally— they are creatures of laws without inner morality. They are not organic, like tribes that feel and revere the same values. They are sheerly instrumental, a pointed arrow aimed at one goal, usually monetary profit. Total subordination of all activity to the status of means is the function of the corporation.

With the development of the computer and voice-image recording, many of the tasks corporations entrusted to persons because some form of human presentation was required (such as giving information, dealing with grievances) can now be dealt with by machines which display the ghosts of persons.

A corporation cannot feel moral obligation, only the pressures of legal compliance. A tape cannot lie to you. The voice recorded is merely an impersonal instrument—like the disembodied lady who intones the minutes and seconds over the phone—instructed to deliver a text written by still another functionary following a policy set by some committee following some protocol in part programmed by some computer. No part of the system bears you ill or love. It cannot lie to you; it can only malfunction.

Regulations and procedures can be planted within the system protocols to keep malfunctions down to a minimum, but there is no way to program a moral ideal like truth into a technical system with technical ends. Truth is a moral value; it is an end in itself; it cannot be the end product of mechanical tinkering.

The modern communications industry, of which broadcasting is the most visible part, is daily becoming more and more one vast interlocking technical system of interfaced corporations. The content of the system is always subservient to some technical purpose like getting votes, ratings, or sales. The process of achieving this purpose is broken down into manageable parts serviced by technicians who have no more identification with the content of what is said or shown than riveters have with auto bodies on assembly lines. Efforts to introduce honesty or truth must be translated into procedures that succeed or fail at making the system more efficient. For the operators of the system, such efforts are invariably seen as troublesome red tape, with no real connection to what they are about. Like pilots forced to make inefficiently patterned approaches and take-offs as part of "noise-abatement procedures," they are quite correct in this assumption.

The concerns of public interest reform groups, like ACT, are putatively moral. But their concerns, to become effective public policy, must be translated into technical rules, which, as we have argued, are essentially amoral.

Two examples of the incompatibility of communications technology and public service immediately spring to mind.

Some years ago there was concern that the "big city" outlook or the "view from Sunset Blvd.," so evident in the majority of programming, should be offset by more local programming. When this policy objective was translated into a regulation, we created the Prime Time Access Rule, which mandated network affiliates to broadcast non-network material from 7:30 to 8:00 PM. The result was that most affiliates bought and broadcast syndicated canned shows or *old* network programs. Very frequently these turned out to be game shows from the limbo of no particular place. Local production would have been less profitable.

Another moral concern is that of access—that groups or viewpoints normally excluded by costs or prejudice be given a chance to mount the national soapbox. A reformist group in California devised a plan for "Free Speech Messages" to be produced along the format lines of commercials or promotional spots. This of course requires that the messages of free speech be delivered with the style and pace of the commercial, a form designed to bypass the reflective mind. Neo-Marxist critiques of our system are put on the podium with Smokey the Bear.

When columnist Jack Anderson irresponsibly publicized a false report that Senator Thomas Eagleton had been arrested for drunken driving, he was called to task and, as a professional person, he both retracted and apologized. But when mistakes or calculated distortions, such as the misleading report of the Vietcong naval assault at Tonkin Gulf or the exaggerated reactions to the Tet offensive, get pumped into the system of interlocking wire services, syndications, and network news departments, no apology, no retraction, no correction is feasible, because no one person ever fully stands behind the report. Like all those ships and planes and gliders on D-Day, a vast and irreversibly mobilized force is in motion. Although the medium may not always be the message, the system has the final say.

No process of purging the media of abuses of the truth can be more than righteous rhetoric without the candid acknowledgement that moral sensitivity and technical planning are at essential odds. Without this, ideals are reduced to ridiculous

rules and the nihilists are made to look like the only honest
people in the room.

THE PUBLIC INTEREST VERSUS SPECIAL INTERESTS

After years of professional observation of the workings of
the federal government, John Herbers of *The New York Times*
compares it to a medieval fair. If you want to get something
done, set up a booth. In a simpler time it could be written that
a proper representative voted according to his conscience
rather than in accord with his constituents, but this was when
differing views were interpreted as divergent understandings
of one overriding public interest. Today special interests are
unabashedly presented as such by professional lobbyists, af-
fording a congressman little time (even if he had the inclination) to ponder a proper balance attentive to the national interest. One does not devise a true energy policy for America. One
reconciles competing special interests, favoring the most
powerfully represented.

The most altruistic statesman would be sorely taxed to propose any realistic and workable policy that genuinely met the
public interest in this pragmatic context. It is clearly in the
public interest, for instance, that every American should have
access to quality health care. It is also clear that no health professional should have access to tax or insurance monies on a
scale that remunerates him fifty to one hundred times the me-
dian national salary. Yet neither of these goals seems within the
grasp of legislators or of regulators. Goals seem to require detailed guidelines that boggle the mind and stifle initiative; controls require multiple layers of bureaucrats to verify and vali-
date services and charges.

Why is this so? Certainly health care, like so many other
things, has become increasingly arcane and complex, but these
characteristics alone cannot account for rocketing costs and
lopsided priorities. The cause is within us: there is no in-
ternalized, naturally felt, culturally sustained personal sense of

right and wrong to override individual opportunism. The law is not for the just man, but for the unjust. The Byzantine administration of our labyrinthine laws is a judgment on our lack of unifying culture and sustaining morality.

In this context, how can the public interest be apprehended, let alone served?

Not too long ago Walter Lippmann defined the public interest as "What men would choose if they saw clearly, thought rationally, acted disinterestedly and benevolently." The guiding framework within which they would see, think, and act Lippmann called "the public philosophy." By this he meant what the scholastics called "the natural law" and the Roman jurists before them, "*jus naturale*." Traditional philosophers considered this to be the rule of reason imposed on all men by their common human nature. Based on thoughtful observation, it is a philosophy; aimed at guiding social behavior, it is public. It is the moral equivalent of Chomsky's "deep structure," from which all mankind devises diverse languages according to preset and universal forms or rules—rules for making rules from the structure of the mind itself. As the structure generates meaningful sentences in any language, the practical reason validates value judgments in any culture. It is no more infallible than language, which can be a vehicle for error; but it is the only framework within which meaning can exist and truth has a chance. Some such supposition of a public philosophy underlay the Allied willingness to prosecute Nazi war criminals according to the Nuremberg Code, an international and universally binding set of basic moral law, which concentration camp practices clearly violated even though those practices were legally correct under locally reigning German law. Although Judge Ford in the trial of the Boston Five refused to accept the validity of the Nuremberg Code as applicable to some of our practices in Vietnam, surely this same implicit presumption of a common human morality bolsters the campaign of Amnesty International against torture and the Carter administration's efforts on behalf of human rights. It moved African leaders to look the other way when French troops helped end the bizarre horrors of Emperor Bokassa, even though Africans would normally protest any military presence of a former colonizing power. There is a public philosophy and it is the window on common and binding morality.

Truth is valued for its own sake in the public philosophy. Telling the truth is therefore "in the public interest" as broadcasting is mandated to be by the Communications Act.

Pilate was bothered by this moral imperative enough to squirm and waffle with his infamous: "What is truth?" as a defense of expediency over honesty. Today, the defense of special interests over the public interest is "Whose truth?" Each booth at the Washington Fair has its own truth to match its private goals.

Within this context of *realpolitik,* media watchdog groups seeking access to the media or fairness from the media in the public interest are relegated to the role of self-serving lobbyists. It would be absurd in this climate to seek truth and justice from the media because both concepts imply a common moral order: a public philosophy that makes the public interest perceptible.

Telecommunications policy, like any public policy, can only be coherently formulated in the light of a perceived and overriding public interest. Public interest springs from an antecedent public philosophy.

Do the broadcast reformers have a public philosophy?

The Public Philosophy versus the Market Model

Reformers and broadcasters seem to vacillate between two conflicting models of the ideal policy for communications. These models flow from implicit assumptions that are irreconcilable at present.

The first model is Public Interest, conceived in the shadow of the natural law as Lippmann invoked it. Those who accept this model believe that there are certain proper goals for broadcasting policy that are unquestionably good, self-evident values. Such would be the American Civil Liberties Union's unswerving dedication to "diversity in programming" as a necessary condition for full and free debate on controversial issues. This view is enshrined in the Fairness Doctrine. The stated goal of the Public Corporation to stimulate regional production at the expense of the concentrated facilities of New York and Los Angeles (if not of London!) is one more such thesis taken as self-evidently correct. The National Citizens Committee on Broadcasting's espousal of greater access for minorities is another certain trumpet. An extreme commitment to the public interest values of diversity, regionalism, and access was put forward by the United States Civil Rights Commission in 1977 and again more strongly in 1979 when it urged the FCC to actively promote programming that "accurately portrays" minorities and women. None of these positions are defended as expedient, useful, or profitable. In board rooms that honor the expedient and profitable, homogeneity, centralization, and relatively elite, "upscale" casting are the rule. These reformist goals spring from a moral vision of what is correct for its own sake: justice, equality, democratic rule. Public order in the public interest derives from the public philosophy.

There is a contrary model for policy that either denies or ignores the moral vision of the reformers. This is the market model. In this context, morality is conceived of as personal and private, never public. One should never "impose one's own morality" on others, who presumably have hermetically sealed moral compartments of their own. This view accepts the public forum as a pit of contention among isolated individuals who must compete for public *attention* by whatever legal means technology affords. There can be no *public* concern for moral uplift, no common worry about corruption of youth, no concerted efforts to stem alleged evil effects of violence or so-called pornography portrayed on the media "irresponsibly," whatever that may mean. Nor is there any eagerness for "controversial issues" receiving adequate coverage for the benefit of the electorate.

Communications is a market, regulated by the impersonal and amoral law of numbers. It is fair as the survival of the fittest is fair: it is the law of nature. If enough numbers cared about minority views, so-called accurate portrayal of racial types, then market forces would inevitably produce them. Congressman Van Deerlin's original (and thus far rejected) proposal for revision of the Communications Act expresses this philosophy when it substitutes "reliable, affordable, efficient" service for "in the public interest, convenience, and necessity" as the guiding light for broadcast policy. Advertisers express the assumptions of the market model when they present commercials as the presentation of information to buyers who are perfectly capable of being beware on their own accounts, without the needless interference of national nannies.

The conflict between the market models and the public interest model of course extends far beyond communications policy. It is a conflict throughout the republic and within each one of us. The public interest model assumes a public philosophy that apprehends some common and universally binding moral order. The market model is practically relativistic: whatever enough people seem to want at this time is fine; tomorrow it may be different; the wheel turns; the wise man anticipates trends. Most people cling to the public interest model when they wish to see a policy implemented: "everyone" should support ERA, the right to an adequate diet among all peoples, abolition of the death penalty, for instance, because these goals are "right." On the other hand, the market model is wonderfully convenient when we do not agree with the moral vision of those who propose something we oppose. Those who wish to outlaw abortion are perfectly free to consider it immoral but they have no right to impose "their morality" on the rest of us. Many sincere people believe mercy killing should be permitted, but most of us fear murderous abuses of such exceptions: "their morality" is admirable—for "them"—but we are not ready for it yet. If this were the early nineteenth century, the abolitionists would be criticized not for trying to free the slaves, but for trying to impose their minority morality on the majority, whose very numbers make them right.

It is evident that a philosophically consistent reformer can never adopt the market model. His interest is the public interest. If only we saw as clearly as he did, thought as rationally, acted as disinterestedly, then we would surely agree with him.

Politically savvy reformers, however, try to avoid the appearance of holding the public philosophy, because our governmental system grants standing to special interests and our constitution is chary of those who wish to save us all from sins we do not quite recognize with the sanctions of the state.

This paradox is best illustrated by the changing tactics of those who oppose pornography. In the past, churches opposed pornography on the clear grounds that it was simply immoral: wrong to make it, wrong to sell it, wrong to enjoy it. It was wrong for everybody because it clearly broke God's laws and offended *common* decency. Many church-affiliated media watchdog groups, such as Morality in Media, still take this stand. Modern and mainstream reformers opposed to pornography, however, find this embarrassing as well as (in their view) ineffective. Thus the even more strident opposition to pornography on the part of feminist groups is endorsed because it is easily digestible as a special interest following the market model: pornography is offensive *to women*.

The same mentality is evident when sound ecological or humanitarian policies are presented as in the best interests of the "rights" of "ignored minorities" like cats, trees, and rocks. Fortunately up to this point many people see such arguments as whimsical.

Finally, there are very pedestrian practical reasons for public interest reformers to sound like special interest or even one-issue lobbyists. In Washington the mechanics of the market work. The biggest booth at the fair gets the most attention. So when the *realpolitik* question, "Whose truth?" is asked, the answer must be: "A large number of active, angry, and bankrolled people." The media watchdogs therefore need money and to get it they must develop loyal supporters. As the American Civil Liberties Union learned to its sorrow when it offended Jews by defending the American Nazis' civil rights to march in Skokie, general ideology is a pale flag next to the blood claims of tribes. Further, the public interest tends to be broad-gauged and long-termed, whereas financial contributors like to see the "bottom line" on the near horizon. Since broadcast responsibility legally resides with local stations, most media reform groups are both local and *ad hoc*. Media revenue and economic organization, however, are national and at times international. Immediately there is a problem of "fit" and proper address for local groups. The ideal form is therefore a national organization with powerful and fiscally sound local chapters that can support the main office. All of these circumstances argue for the certain appeal of special interest campaigns to achieve what are genuinely perceived by the reformers to be public interest goals.

Intellectual consistency argues for a frank adoption of the public philosophy. Political circumstances require a loyal constituency that can pay for the group and influence Congress. But the market model never leads to lasting reform, as abolitionists of the past, and the Marxists and "born-again" Christians of today know very well.

Positive Freedom versus Negative Freedom

To follow the tactics of the market while adhering to the ideals of the public philosophy is not necessarily to be involved in absolute contradiction, but it creates formidable obstacles to coherent policy. And it must be emphasized that consistent policy is not merely an intellectual luxury; it is the ultimate political imperative. American foreign affairs, fiscal management, and energy problems are all testimonies to the price paid for a policy vacuum.

In the context of telecommunications policy and the public interest, Isaiah Berlin's distinction between positive and negative freedom is a useful intellectual tool for diagnosing the essence of the inconsistency.

Positive freedom, for Berlin, is an inner spiritual reality. It is the capacity to choose the better thing, at times the best thing, according to some moral vision or religious ideal. It is the freedom to want what one should. Negative freedom, as he stipulates it, is merely the absence of external constraints on our outer behavior that can be imposed by our fellow humans. Mahatma Gandhi, in jail, enjoyed a high degree of positive freedom even while he was deprived of negative freedom. Charles Manson, before his arrest, enjoyed negative freedom while confined by his compulsions to a very low order of positive freedom. Negative freedom is the freedom to do whatever you want.

Martin Luther King, preaching at the Washington Mall, experienced both freedoms. A drugged and broken spirit in a Soviet psychiatric hospital knows neither freedom.

For Berlin it is evident that positive freedom is the more noble concept of human potential. Negative freedom is merely a condition which can come to good only if positive freedom is also present. For that very reason, Berlin insists, positive freedom should never be a *political* goal. The state should never be the arbiter of what one should want. The state should exist merely to give the maximum negative freedom to each by imposing the minimum necessary restraints on all. Those who believe the state should repeal laws against "victimless crimes" are implicitly following this view. The state should not be an arbiter of internal morality, a big brother sent to guide us and punish us if we deviate from the good and the true "for our own good." The state as the guarantor of negative freedom is merely the referee commissioned to prevent foul play.

Soviet psychiatry, Maoist Thought Reform, and the Spanish Inquisition all presented themselves as enhancing human freedom by helping people to want what they should—positive freedom. In its name, virtually all negative freedom can be withheld.

Outside the realm of politics, however, positive freedom is precisely what all of us should strive for. People who voluntarily sign up for Weight Watchers or Smokenders, Transcendental Meditation or Trappist monastery life, Olympic training or law school are doing just that.

The censor invariably sees positive freedom as a political ideal. He wishes the state to guide citizens to want what they should by shielding them from temptations to want what they should not, according to the philosophy or religion of the censor. Behind this wish is also the implicit division of mankind into the correct and mature and the immature and incorrect.

For centuries printed material contained the bawdy and lubricious, from the *Ars Amatoria* to limericks. With the development of the high speed press and the growth of literacy, the Victorians feared for the morality of the uneducated masses who might be corrupted by the material. At the turn of the century Americans were horrified that unlettered immigrants would be corrupted by the "picture show." The "Principles" of the original Hollywood *Production Code* make it clear that movies, since they are seen by many ordinary people, must be more strictly censored than the Broadway theater of sophisticated playgoers. You must want what you should. Compared to the educated elite, the mass of people are as children. The state must care for them.

In seeking access for themselves or for ignored minorities, the media watchdogs seem to be espousing the market concept of competition for attention. The state is needed to impose minimum restraints on exclusionary policies by monopolies or oligopolies. Without state protection, they cannot do what they want. In this sense the market model follows the ideal of negative freedom.

In seeking diversity, accurate portrayal of racial minorities, and fairness, the watchdogs seem to want the state to protect citizens from bad ideas and harmful influences. The state must endorse "correct" positions. People must be educated to want what they should by the state. This is to convert the public interest into positive freedom as a *political* ideal.

Keeping within Berlin's framework, one is nevertheless not forced to adopt the market model as superior to the public philosophy. For Berlin the positive freedom needed to pursue the public interest is a superior ideal. But it is a dangerous *political* ideal. Ideals can be socially promoted and culturally sanctioned without recourse to regulatory agencies.

CULTURAL CONTROLS VERSUS LEGAL RESTRAINTS

Motion pictures once occupied the center stage of media concern and were the focus of moral outrage and hopes for educating the masses. A parallel to the current efforts of public interest groups to influence broadcast programming was the national effort to control the content of the movies. The effort began before 1916 in Chicago, which had a municipal censorship board (with policemen serving on it) and lasted until 1967, when Jack Valenti of the Motion Picture Association presided over the revision of the Motion Picture Production Code and the introduction of film classification ("Rated PG"). From beginning to end there was great antipathy to state control, which never materialized beyond the local level, and which was eliminated at that level by alternate control pressures from the private sector.

Among all these pressures the most focused, the most effective, and the most controversial was that brought to bear by the Legion of Decency. The Legion began in the thirties with prodigious fanfare and died a quiet death in the middle sixties by being transformed into a rather differently oriented entity, the National Catholic Office for Motion Pictures.

In the thirties as today, films were not regulated directly by any government agency. There was nevertheless a serious possibility that some form of national film censorship might be inaugurated to meet grass-roots outrage at the alleged immorality of films. Some states were already impaneling film review boards. As early as 1907 Chicago had passed a censorship law directed at the naughty nickelodeon and by 1929 more than 48 bills had been introduced in state legislatures to control film distribution and exhibition. The heartland of America perceived the "flappers in flivvers" of the roaring twenties as a moral degeneration of American values and saw the film industry as a promoter of this degeneration, which it felt originated in New York and Hollywood. In those days regionalism was a conservative property. In 1922 the trade association of the film producers and distributors set up a public relations operation and put a former Postmaster General, Will Hays, in the director's chair. His task was to clear the name and clean the image of the industry.

Hays felt that local and regional censorship was killing sales. Films approved by one state board would be condemned by another on unpredictable grounds. In 1919 the Pennsylvania board had banned 16 films already approved by other boards. Hays sent out representatives to canvass the various regions and find out their grounds for objecting to films. When his emissaries came back, Hays compiled the complaints into a laundry list he called "Don'ts and Be Carefuls" and circulated it among the studios, which could censor their scripts before shooting to avoid distribution tie-ups after costly production was completed. The 11 "Don'ts" were strictly forbidden: licentious nudity, drug traffic, white slavery, profane language, willful offense to any nation, race, or creed, ridicule of the clergy, scenes of childbirth or children's genitals, sex hygiene, miscegenation, and sex perversion. The 24 "Be Carefuls" included the use of the American flag, methods of perpetrating crimes, and legal executions. The list was obviously based on precedent, not principle, and offered no certain immunity from censorship difficulties. Hays and his employers quite obviously looked upon the film industry as a business first and an art second. Film was cut the way suits were—you want two pairs of pants, you get two pairs of pants. The customer was always right. It is interesting that censorship is returning today in the same guise, with the modern concept of consumer protection.

As with the variety of *ad hoc* and local watchdog groups today, different regions and cities objected to different kinds of material. Hays' list was a makeshift response to what promised to be an enduring and worsening problem for the film business. If only there were some way to *centralize* and *certify* objections that might lead to costly exhibition bans and to make these objections known *before* money was spent on production.

The need of the film industry for a reliable pre-production code with uniform provisions for the entire nation and the localized frustrations of bourgeois moralists who regarded each new film as a fresh assault on the innocence and integrity of the American home presented themselves to Martin Quigley, Sr., as a golden opportunity to do good and to do well. Quigley knew the business; he was publisher of the *Motion Picture Herald.* He was also a Roman Catholic and a family man. He approached a member of the Chicago Motion Picture Censorship Commission, Rev. Fitzgeorge Dineen, S.J., and presented the moral desirability of a uniform code as a means to stop evil at the source, as it were. . . . Dineen called in a fellow Jesuit, Dan Lord, who had served as a "technical adviser" for the original *King of Kings,* to assist Quigley in drawing up a code.

Quigley then presented the code to Hays as the answer to the industry's problems. On March 31, 1930, one year after Quigley made the original suggestion to Dineen, the Motion Picture Producers and Distributors adopted Quigley's code as their own, after Hays had incorporated some of his laboriously acquired "Don'ts and Be Carefuls."

Hollywood saw the Production Code, as it came to be known, as an advisory service to aid marketing. There had been no enforcement provision in its adoption and distributors in metropolitan areas where censorship was not a problem felt free to ignore it. Quigley was well aware that adoption was but the first step. There must be social enforcement. It was therefore fortunate that he had enlisted two Roman Catholic clergymen to inaugurate his plans. The Catholic Church with its admirable organization could well serve as the cadre for a national grass-roots movement that would endorse the Code and back it with boycotts. No Code compliance, no tickets sold.

Quigley and the Jesuits enlisted members of the Catholic hierarchy through the fine offices of the Rector of the Catholic University in Washington, D.C., and the Apostolic Delegate from Rome. The movement gained momentum and garnered the membership of 54 separate organizations, including the Protestant Federal Council of Churches of Christ in America (membership of 20 million), the United Presbyterian Assembly, the National Conference of Christians and Jews, and an editorial endorsement from *The New York Times* on July 13, 1934.

A key figure in the campaign was public relations man Joseph I. Breen of the Peabody Coal Company and a friend of Quigley who had been impressed by his performance as publicity coordinator for the Catholic Eucharistic Congress at Chicago in 1925. When Hollywood capitulated to the campaign and formed the Production Code Administration to enforce the Code with fines and hired professional censor-consultants to advise producers at the script stage on how to avoid fines, Breen was brought in by Hays to run the operation. Breen stayed on for 20 years and took his job seriously, although he developed a reputation for flamboyant humor.

The movement thus became institutionalized by a professional office funded by the industry it was to police. Alone, this would have been no more effective than the current National Association of Broadcasters Code Authority. In New York the Catholic hierarchy established a permanent office of their own for boycotting any films that failed to live up to their interpretation of the Code. This required large-scale monitoring of films, a practice that is central to most of the public interest groups today with regard to television. Like today's groups, the Legion depended on volunteers and these volunteers were mostly Catholic laywomen who had attended a Catholic college (women are disproportionately represented in monitoring activities of television today as well). In the early forties this group was supplemented by male consultants, lay and clergy. In the late fifties the original homogeneous group of Catholic alumnae were finally supplanted by a much larger number of consultants, with a slight male majority. Whereas the Code Administration either granted or withheld a seal of approval, the Legion classified films according to their acceptability.

The Legion opened in New York on February 1, 1936. In its first year and a half, 1,271 films were reviewed of which 13 were condemned; 98 were found partially objectionable and 360 suitable only for adults. There was a gentlemen's agreement between the coasts that a classification might be upgraded if certain scenes were omitted or modified. Hollywood censors warned producers that certain scenes would "never get by New York" and they were dutifully modified.

What standards or criteria did Legion reviewers apply? In addition to the Code itself, which the industry had accepted, there was a great deal of unofficial reliance on "The Morals of the Screen," an article by Richard Dana Skinner for the October, 1935, *Catholic Educational Review*. Both Skinner and the Code made an important distinction between what they called "theme" and "treatment." The former is the central idea of the film while the latter is all the thousands of details of physical presentations. As with many media watchdogs today, the Legion was far more concerned with appearances than with ideas. From 1956 to 1966, for instance, the Legion objected to "suggestive costumes" 257 times, but to "amoral philosophy" 16 times. In this the Legion foreshadowed the current preoccupation with statistics and the "violence index" used to judge the acceptability of television fare. So when it comes to making moral judgments about technical artifacts that are mass produced, even in so artistic a form as the film, there is an inescapable flight to technical rules; morality is measured in inches of thigh exposed. This turned out to be true even among those so ostensibly interested in the "soul" of the audience. Nonetheless, the force of the Legion was cultural, not legal, not through regulatory government agencies with punitive state powers.

As a cultural control, the Legion-Code connection was able to bend with the times. As the sixties progressed, both the industry authority and the Church authority began to wither, for economic reasons and due to social revolution. The less than one dozen reviewers of the Code Administration found their recommendations ignored and later not sought in the first place. The Legion could not keep anyone, not even Catholics, from attending movies that advertising had effectively promoted. If the Code had been applied by some "Federal Film Commission," their civil service inspectors could hardly be dismissed and one can imagine the number of directives and lawsuits that would have been generated. As it was, when the Code was formally simplified and classification was introduced in 1967, it had long ceased to be applied at all. To paraphrase *My Fair Lady,* the current revised Code allows anything at all so long as it is classified properly. The National Catholic Film Office of today is primarily an educational office, seeking to promote films that are provocative of moral judgments on the human condition, as the Office sees it.

In the first wave of media watching, groups like the Legion *assumed* cultural commitments to certain moral values and set out to *protect* those commitments from assault by media representations that showed "sin" (whose evil was self-evident) in an attractive light. It was a mobilizing force for the existing attitudes of the middle class. A reading of the Production Code makes it clear that the political *status quo* was also protected. Judges, policemen, clergymen, and other authority figures were never to be portrayed in dramatic situations which would cast their righteousness, as a class, in doubt. Sexy or politically satiric films were viewed as coming straight from the devil's workshop. Later on, in the sixties, the waning of this cultural confidence permitted the emergence of toleration for films like *Doctor Strangelove* and *Midnight Cowboy*.

Did the Legion "impose its own morality" on the rest of us? No. It imposed our own morality on us. Anyone who asserts that the Legion was some sinister force for "Catholic dogma" simply has not taken the trouble to look at what the record shows. The Legion imposed the bland formulas of middle American bourgeois values for as long as they represented the mainstream. Since the new code has come into being new formulas of sadistic brutality and sexploitation have taken over. The Legion made it all the more inevitable for the FBI and GI Joe to be seen as virtually flawless and for communism, drugs, and extramarital sex to be presented as robbing America of its vital juices. The only Catholicism Hollywood ever pushed was the bland goodiness of Bing Crosby and Barry Fitzgerald, which was of a piece with screenwriters' saccharin stereotypes of all ministers and rabbis—a sort of *Reader's Digest* melange of lovable codgers and untainted youths whose very ignorance of the world was a warm and winning trait. Perhaps they might have done better to present attractive images of Catholicism, much as the Jewish organizations discouraged Shylock stereotypes and promoted films, like *Gentleman's Agreement,* which rightly stigmatized anti-Semitism. In any event, it is arguable that today special interest groups through the sought-for *legal* pressures of the FCC and the Civil Rights Commission are trying to extend privileges of clergy to blacks, cops, homosexuals, doctors, and American Indians, whenever they are portrayed on television.

The Legion focused existing majority prejudices and thus

made impossible to produce what was already unlikely to be filmed. Both the industry and the mainstream audiences that the Legion had represented in its flourishing period agreed that official government intervention would be unconstitutional and dangerous.

The wheel has turned. Today's watchdogs see the government as their partner against the corporate establishment. Now the division is not between the conservative bourgeois and the radical artists, but between the capitalists and the workers, the producers and the consumers, the parents and the professionals. The Legion never criticized the *structure* of the film industry because it was beyond the cultural consciousness of the times to see structure as determining content. If anything, the Legion favored the hegemony of a few large studios because it centralized control and favored conservatism. When the structure did change, both the Code and the Legion began to lose clout.

Current media watchers are many and varied but none approach the strength of the Legion in the early years of its interfaith coalition support. Some, like the National Federation for Decency or Morality in Media, are more conservative and more concerned with sex than the Legion had been. Some are more "hip" and liberal, like ACT or the National Citizens Committee for Broadcasting. None of the groups shares the luxury of common cultural support, of an assured *common* decency, upon which the Legion could securely depend to push its version of positive liberty: the sacredness of the family, the importance of internal sanctions for obeying laws and respecting *status quo* authority. After the Civil Rights Movement, Vietnam, and Watergate, the model for virtue has become anti-establishment and the one unquestioned assumption is that any idea or value is entitled to a media forum provided it has some special interest constituency. The family and institutions are no longer sacred. The individual is now centrally sacred; equal opportunity for disadvantaged groups is not focused on the groups, but on each individual who has the personal trait of being a member of such a group. The context of the lobbying activity of modern media watchers reinforces the modern awareness of the individual as a solitary focus of rights and needs within a monolithic state, as opposed to the Legion consensus directed toward families and groups that must preserve and protect their moral traditions, with scrupulous independence from any state interference. The Legion existed in a world of *meanings,* however naive. Public interest media groups share a world of individuals who experience *effects.*

The Legion safely assumed that people were influenced by what they saw and heard, especially if it were presented with vivid dramatic impact. ACT's concerns occur at a time when such assumptions can be ruled out of court as "unscientific" and "impressionistic." Elaborate "studies" must thus be trotted out to "prove" some *physical effect* on viewers. Like tooth decay. Higher blood pressure, doll punching, adolescent rape are some of the alleged and very varied effects cited by such studies as undesirable effects. These are "facts" rather than meanings or influences.

As constituents of Boorstin's Republic of Technology, each individual has a right to be spared the deleterious effects of these facts, which are statistically associated with television programming of a certain type. The government, then, as arbiter of last resort and traffic manager of isolated individuals pursuing their own Millsian good in their own way, must make rules to eliminate certain types of programming that have been "scientifically proven" to be associated with undesirable *effects.*

Cultural controls have been replaced by legal restraints. The alleged imposition of morality has been replaced by technical rules. On June 9, 1978, the United States Civil Rights Commission formally requested the Federal Communications Commission to investigate "the network programming decision-making process and the resulting . . . underrepresentation and stereotyping of minorities and women in television drama." The Commission further recommended that the FCC investigate "the effects on both majority and minority viewers of underrepresentation and stereotyping." So far the FCC has refused on constitutional grounds.

A particular version of positive freedom is being sought as a political ideal.

6 – *The Public Interest and the Educated Heart*

THE BRANSCOMB-SAVAGE SURVEY OF selected media watchdog groups makes a number of recommendations intended to aid the accomplishment of their various missions. There is one recommendation that is repeated again and again: the need for valid research.

Although the survey never spells out exactly why this is desirable, it is clear to anyone conversant with the context of media watching that different groups accuse the media of being too right wing (The Network Project) or too left wing (Accuracy in Media); of being sexist (N.O.W. Media Task Force) and of being sexy (Morality in Media); of being too adult-oriented (ACT) or of not offering enough mature content (National Citizens Committee for Broadcasting). For every charge there is a countercharge and the media themselves can well afford to sponsor the most expensive audience research and then package it most attractively for the public and their politicians. The Civil Rights Commission Report for 1979 shows great respect for the argumentative power of research: it offers extensive content analysis, with many tables of percentages and figures for minority roles on network television. The Report goes so far as to list by name each female network correspondent with the number of minutes and the number of times each has been on the air, both absolutely and as a percentage of total correspondent time.

It is assumed by Branscomb-Savage that there exists some formula for research that will yield the "real facts" and thus end argument with evidence. Realistically it is granted that he who pays the piper calls the tune, so an independent research service institution is recommended as serving all groups on some sort of democratic basis.

Of course there is no such thing as a "true" research picture in survey research involving opinion statements. Every bit of research has philosophical and political presuppositions, be it laboratory research in a psychological testing institute or field surveys of ever increasing sample sizes. Functional research is not value-free; it is just inarticulate or silent about the values it serves, while presenting reams of subjectively constructed "data." It is to the credit of the FCC, in replying to the Civil Rights Commission's requests to "investigate" programming, that it stated:

> We believe that the conclusions drawn by the CCR from the stated compilations (="research") cannot be readily accepted without an analysis of the actual programs monitored and an assessment of the subjective determinations made by the monitors.
> (Letter of Wallace E. Johnson, FCC Broadcast Bureau Chief, to Mr. Louis Nunez, CCR Acting Staff Director, October 16, 1978.)

There is simply no scientific way to get from 'is' to 'ought' and properly conducted research of any kind can only indicate what is from one specific viewpoint. Most of the "research" tables in the Civil Rights Commission Report were derived from a two-week monitoring period; had they been derived from 20 years of carefully annotated viewing, they would still leave one with a mountain of impressions dressed up as facts.

Real science, let alone pseudo-science, is no substitute for the public philosophy. The latter springs from the disinterested study of human history and the enlightened use of practical judgment to decide on the best *moral* course: that which serves the preservation of civilized values in social life. The former merely measures observations without any accountability for the point of view or the criteria of variable selection.

A stunning yet average example of the manipulation of survey research from the opposite quarter was the Roper Organization's *Public Perceptions of Television and Other Mass Media: A Twenty Year Review 1959–1978* published by the Television Information Office (TIO) in April of 1979. The TIO is the public relations arm of the National Association of Broadcasters for television. Studies of this type are commissioned annually and provide handy statistics for convention speeches and sales pitches. Because of the ACT-instigated overtures of the FTC to control children's commercials, the study gave particular attention to this area.

The survey asked parents of children aged three to ten (note the age bracket) if their little ones could distinguish between commercials and regular programming. As one might suppose, 89% said their children could tell the difference. (Do you think my kid is a dummy?); 79% said their children were aware of the selling purpose of commercials. The calculated naivete of these questions is only exceeded by the intensity of motivational research that goes into the construction of commercials for children and adults.

In the same study an even more predictable response was elicited on a subject most sensitive for broadcast owners:

> In your judgment, which one or two of the people or groups on this list should have the most to say about what (news reports, entertainment programs, commercials) people see and hear on television?
> —The individual viewers by deciding what they will and will not watch?
> —The television networks and stations by deciding what they will and will not put on the air?
> —The advertisers by deciding what they will and will not sponsor?

—The Federal Government by deciding what can and cannot be put on the air?

—Social action and religious groups by recommending what should and should not be on the air?

As this study presented the alternatives, there is not much doubt about the outcome. Either the respondent (the person asked the question by the researchers) is in charge (he is "the individual") or somebody else is. This is the Roper translation for the existing industry yardstick, the ratings. One might construct a similar bit of survey research for the National Petroleum Institute, or the Edison Institute: Who should control the rates of electrical utilities? Why the individual, of course, by deciding whether or not he wants to pay for electricity. The individual is also in charge of the price of gasoline, by deciding whether or not he wants to pay the larcenous levy at the pump. This is the market model stripped of even the slightest public interest modifications. The answers (="facts from reliable research") are: 71% chose the individual; 26%, the networks and stations; 12%, the advertisers; 9%, the federal government; and 9%, social action and religious groups—the exact ranking in which the schedule listed them! Others have documented the meretricious use of survey research, among them Michael Wheeler from the outside and Seymour Martin Lipset from the inside; we merely wish to point to the abuses relevant to our discussion.

As one of the more "hip" media watchdogs, ACT has commissioned research of its own and more groups would do it if they had the money or the grantswomanship of Peggy Charren. This is understandable, but it is tragic. It is an unnecessary concession that only "experts" are gifted with insight into the effect of drama, news, and literature; this is merely to substitute accountants for critics. Relying on putative research is a distrust of common sense. Executives out of their depth generally fly to procedures from matters of substance in order to look busy and decisive when they don't know what to do. If public interest groups argue that research reports are necessary as ammunition at government hearings, then they are becoming part of the problem by conceding the field to the iron triangle in place: regulatory agencies, congressional committees, and lobbyists delight in the apparatus of survey research and handsomely reproduced reports of begged questions.

In such complex policy questions as energy production, credit regulation, and natural resource management, technical studies are indispensable and appropriate. Is this also true of our sense of what is nourishing or damaging to the minds and hearts of our children? Are we so lacking in cultural confidence, so dependent on doctors and psychiatrists to reassure us about everyday life, that we have substituted experts and putative research for the moral monopoly formerly accorded professional holy men?

Master manipulators know how to play on this insecurity even as they deny its existence. On the one hand, apologists for no-holds-barred advertising assert that the public can judge the reliability and informational value of commercials for itself, without any handholding from would-be do-gooders. On the other hand, the same apologists dismiss criticism of advertising as amateurish complaints unsubstantiated by requisite, and arcane, research. Programming and commercials are always aimed at "individuals" whereas criticism always comes from "social action and religious groups." As an individual, free and franchised, you do not need any research to accept whatever is sent your way by motivational or market research. If you complain, it is as a member of a group, which could not possibly know enough to justify complaints and is probably just trying to "impose its own morality" on the country, which consists of "individuals" served by responsive government and responsible corporations. General Motors, we are told as an instance, is really just "people serving other people." This usefully warm phrase aptly describes every social arrangement from the service at Maxim's to the underground labor in the South African Rand. In the realm beyond rhetoric, however, some people are more screwed than served by other people. If they object to such treatment, they had best do so as members of a strong group with the mettle to make it within those very tough iron triangles.

Pseudo-scientific survey research, while it may be an effective instrument for justifying bureaucratic decisions (thus based on "facts" rather than "opinions"), can hardly serve as a guide for *judgment*. Presenting "reports" may be a way to get *action* for a proposal, but it is hardly the means toward formulating the policy to be proposed. The intellectual contradictions between the market model of communications and the public philosophy of communications confuse judgments and befuddle policy formulations. In the end, the value of any media watchdog group's contribution to the national level of civilization lies in the critical judgments it makes on existing programming and in the creative judgments made by artists and entrepreneurs in response to those critical judgments.

As already noted, the public philosophy is not some set of crystal-clear principles that need only be memorized. It is a moral "deep structure" that generates judgments in a way analogous to the sentence generation of linguistic deep structure. Many men speak a vast variety of languages and different people have different things to say, but all language is a vehicle for meaning. Gifted individuals contribute striking adaptations of language to clothe new and intricate insights, which then become the heritage of later users of language on which they in turn build. So it is with moral conscience and aesthetic judgment. As the ability to craft sentences can be enhanced by education and exposure to the masters of language, to the poets, so too can the ability to evaluate and criticize be refined and developed by exposure to the masters of judgment, to the philosophers and artists. Language education does not make everyone say the same thing, but it does enable people to communicate with sensitivity and exactitude what they have in mind. Education of the heart does not make us feel the same things, but it does enable us to connect what we feel with the measured and sophisticated judgments of our heritage and our traditions.

The educated heart is the repository of the public philosophy and the link between the individual, the ultimate seat of all judgment, and groups, the only source for objectivity, fairness, and truth. Communication is only conceivable within a community so that "social action and religious groups" may be validated by their participation in the larger human society, which the great teachers of our heritage have seen as a global *family*. "The individual" of tendentious survey research is an isolated atom, jolted by stimuli and scampering along the corridors of the managed corporate state. In the humanistic tradition, each person is a microcosm within the cosmos, an ordered and ordering organism that reflects, and reflects on, the order around him. His judgments are the social and historical acts of a free and thinking member of a community. The larger the community and the more broad its horizons, the more sensitive and fruitfully exquisite are the judgments and choices made by its participants. Certain individuals are gifted judges and we particularly benefit from their originality and insight. In this order of things, values are not arbitrarily concocted by "interest groups," they are discovered and articulated from the shared moral consciences of men, who devise laws and institutions to preserve these values.

Without totally sharing the despairing diagnosis of Christopher Lasch, we must admit that much of our trouble can be conveniently summarized as "the culture of narcissism." Many Americans are self-obsessed lonely individuals who want the warmth of tribe without commitment to community, who want the comforts of technology without the demands of civilization. Our communication system is a reflection and a reinforcement of this collective narcissism; if not the cause of our malaise, it is a spectacular symptom. Narcissists are easily manipulated: tell them they are individuals and hand them opinions they are taught to believe are their own.

Academic hacks love to point out the patent superficialities of mass culture. Assuredly, the lyrics of Bob Dylan are no substitute for the dialogues of Plato, but it was the academics who brought Dylan and Disney into the sacred grove. Teachers have succumbed to the mass-produced lesson and have been sold mass-produced teaching packages the way families have been sold convenience foods. The automatic version was an advance in mechanical devices, why not in our cultural customs? Thus did hearts cease to be educated.

If the television set and the radio have become the fountainheads of authority in the home, the student center, frequently the most lavish building on campuses for the last 20 years, has become the shrine of mass culture on university territory, where the public philosophy and the possibility of the educated heart have been sold out. Instead of the faculties educating students into our traditions, they have flocked with them to mass culture celebrities who are paid enormous sums to present live and in person what is already available on a 24-hour basis. Educators and parents who have relied on the convenient automatisms of mass culture for the past generations can hardly engage in jeremiads against the shallowness and incompetencies of what they have created.

The educated heart and the public philosophy are waiting for the schools and universities, as intellectual and moral communities rather than as information service stations, to revive them.

7 – The Future of
Public Interest Media Watching

SOME OBSERVERS BELIEVE THAT WE ARE on the verge of a technological revolution in communications that will drastically alter the structure of broadcasting and thus of its moral and cultural impact. Videodiscs, home videocording, megacapacity satellite (for the long haul) and optical fiber cable (for the short haul) transmission systems, the interchangeability of print and audiovisual display formats, holography, microstorage systems, computer-commanded switching systems—all these technologies, it is believed, will put an end to *broad*casting and usher in an era of *narrow*casting. This means that each group can be served exactly the style and substance of communication that it desires, without being "forced" to take broadcast fare that offends its sensibilities. Individuals will be able to read or experience sound-with-image at their own place and pace. Television and radio are the principal vehicles for *mass* media whereas books and some magazines are private media. The new narrowcasting will extend privacy to the electronic. In this system the individual does seem to be in control, as he most definitely is not in the broadcast system, which thus is under some necessity to serve the public interest.

In the envisaged world of narrowcasting, the public interest media watchdogs would have no legal standing nor moral purchase on the industry. The market model guarantees that if there is a teeming multiplicity of narrowcast choices all interests will be served. Minority tastes and views might cost more but this is already true in the non-regulated publishing business, which no one suggests is offending the public interest.

The new technologies free individuals from the restraints of central scheduling and increase the privatization that began with writing and expanded with print, but they do not bring with them the gift of logic and disciplined thinking that writing so enhanced. Fragmented modern society will be deprived of even the artificial glue of mass media broadcasting. The public interest will vanish.

Many observers feel that, quite to the contrary, the new technologies will serve as direct stimuli to public debate, democratic government, and consumer representation. This is because the new systems permit interaction, two-way communications, *feedback*. Warner Communications' trial Qube cable system in the Midwest already has given its subscribers the opportunity to register their views and see them instantly tabulated for public discussions of matters of local and even national interest.

"Feedback," appropriately, is an engineering concept. It describes self-regulating mechanisms, like thermostatically controlled heating and cooling or automobile cruise control. Sensors detect speed, temperature, or any other measurable physical reality, and transmit a numeric value for the reality to the proper device so that it can adjust its output to the preset value, like 68 degrees Fahrenheit or 55 miles per hour. Feedback is essentially a device to control what is being measured. Although very slow, survey research commissioned by merchants and politicians is a form of feedback. The responses inform them of what is working and what isn't, so that strategies can be adjusted. "Do you agree that there is a shortage of oil? Strongly? You disagree? Strongly? Perhaps you are not sure?"

This kind of question can be asked and no doubt will be asked on a national scale. The new technologies merely multiply and extend the tone and effect of Johnny Carson asking his audience for a show of hands to indicate approval of the ecology of downtown Burbank. It is either a diversion or a device for social control: a gimmick. Like the early writing of Socrates' time, it creates the illusion of dialogue while making the real thing less likely.

The colossal marketing potential of the new technologies has already affected the old narrowcast book trade by making economies of scale more attractive than ever. As a result, more and more books are being produced with less variety of content, imitating broadcasting with massive printings and rapid turnover for shorter stock lists.

Thus, even as the watchdogs lose legal leverage over a regulated medium, they must increase their efforts to serve the public interest and influence the new communications to do so. There is no reason to believe that market forces will naturally shape new media toward meeting the educational and entertainment and political needs of the using public more than they influenced old style broadcasting. The market model militates against the diversity, regionalism, and cultural quality that should characterize public media because it reduces the content of communications to the output of a high technology system. It must make end results, from eating tomatoes to reading novels, subservient to the technical process itself.

Fortunately, at least outside of communications, there is growing general distrust of massive centralization. Despite the obstacles against them, co-ops, communes, and collectives have increased in the seventies without the adolescent hoopla of the "counterculture." The establishment argument against communalism is that it is theoretically beautiful but practically unproductive and inefficient. If one wants the same things from communes and small, intermediate technologies that large centralized systems provide, the argument holds. The solitary urban individual, if he is one of the fortunate few on some permanent work force, with health insurance, a guaranteed wage, and a pension plan (even after he has worked almost six months to pay taxes) can be supplied with a home computer that will turn his lights on and off and pay his bills on time, with a home entertainment center bringing celebrities to his air-conditioned personal space. He is guaranteed a rising standard of consumption, provided the centralized system is kept globally secure by atomic threats.

It is no longer the long-haired soapbox orators who decry the system for providing enforced truces without meaningful peace, chemical mood enhancers without peace of mind, propaganda and distraction in place of enlightenment and entertainment, the abandoned responsibilities of the arts, universities, and churches. Public interest media watchers should be concentrating on this latter condition, as other consumer and political action groups address the other problems of our creaking system. The new technologies do not overcome the centralizing narcosis of the present broadcast establishment; they merely make responsibility harder to pinpoint.

Dispersed individuals making purchasing decisions under the influence of centralized advertising campaigns are certainly *not* in charge of the system. In 1975 the United States Census Bureau reported that over 22 per cent of all American households have but a single occupant. If we add the institutionalized who have semi-private to private facilities to the number of Americans who are alone and who will be relying on the new technologies as their window on reality, the power of the image producers is enormous, broad- or narrowcast.

Only strong face-to-face group identity defends against propaganda. The steel squad structure of the Wehrmacht made it reasonably strong in the face of Allied propaganda and overwhelming odds. This same strength characterized the Turkish contingent in the U.N. forces during the Korean War—they proved embarrassingly superior to Americans when captured and "brainwashed." The Amish and other long established tightly-knit groups successfully resist, for good and for ill, the centralizing pressures of corporate and government propaganda. Not being members of the mass, they are not much influenced by the media.

Public interest media watchdogs and each one of us in this

painful period of cultural and economic transformation face an acute dilemma: In order to become more fully human, we must share in the ideals of a group with values and traditions. Since so many of us are cut off from such nourishing groups, we fall back on the packaged values produced by government and corporations to keep us functioning as obedient and predictable citizen-consumers. Opting out of this mass conformism is difficult and can take on the fearful coloration of fanatical cults, like that of tragic Jonestown, which frighten people into greater withdrawal. This isolation in turn leads to still greater dependence on the privatizing media that provide the illusory fellowship of consumption communities, from the Pepsi Generation to Volvo Owners.

At such a time we must be grateful for any truly *public* effort to form groups to serve the *public* interest. Effective service requires deep acquisition of the public philosophy.

Public interest media watchers must be in touch not only with the technical procedure of *getting what they want*—lobbying expertise and production savvy for making "effective" media messages of their own—they must also be in touch with the public philosophy so that they will *know what they should want*. The public interest must serve the larger human family and not merely some factitious "interest group" or ethnic atavism.

If this is not done, if there are no educated hearts among the public interest groups, then we only have special interests seeking by technical means the limited ends of people who know themselves only as consumers and not as human agents of change and patients of beauty and wonder.

———

Selective Bibliography for Part Two

Berlin, Sir Isaiah. "Two Concepts of Liberty," from *Four Essays on Liberty*. New York: Oxford University Press, 1969. Pp. 118–172.

Boorstin, Daniel J. *The Republic of Technology*. New York: Harper & Row, 1978.

Branscomb, Anne W., and Maria Savage. *Broadcast Reform at the Crossroads*. Cambridge, Mass.: Kalba Bowen Associates, 1978.

Chomsky, Noam. *Syntactic Structures*. Hawthorne, N.Y.: Mouton, 1957, 1977.

Draves, Pamela. Ed. *Citizens Media Directory*. Washington, D.C.: National Citizens Committee for Broadcasting, 1977.

Forster, E. M. "The Machine Stops," from *The Eternal Moment and Other Stories*. New York: Harcourt, Brace, 1928.

Herbers, John. "Washington: An Insider's Game." *New York Sunday Times Magazine,* April 22, 1979. Pp. 33 ff.

Homet, Roland S., Jr. "The Future of Public-Interest Law," from Theodore J. Schneyer and Frank Lloyd, *The Public Interest Media Reform Movement: A Look at the Mandate and a New Agenda*. Washington, D.C.: Aspen Institute for Humanistic Studies, 1976. P. 25.

Lasch, Christopher. *The Culture of Narcissism: American Life in an Age of Diminishing Expectations*. New York: W. W. Norton, 1978.

Lasswell, Harold. "Nations and Classes: Symbols of Identification," from Bernard Berelson and Morris Janowitz (eds.), *Reader in Public Opinion and Communication*. 2nd ed. New York: The Free Press, 1966.

Lifton, Robert Jay. *Thought Reform and the Psychology of Totalism*. New York: W. W. Norton, 1963.

Lippmann, Walter. *Essays in the Public Philosophy*. Boston: Little, Brown, 1955.

Lipset, Seymour Martin, and William Schneider. "Polls for the White House and the Rest of Us," *Encounter* 49 No. 5 (November 1977) pp. 24–34.

Phelan, John M. *An Investigation of the Policy and Practice of Film Classification*. New York University. Unpublished Ph.D. dissertation, 1968.

———. *Mediaworld: Programming the Public*. New York: Seabury/Continuum Books, 1977.

The Roper Organization. *Public Perceptions of Television and Other Mass Media: A Twenty Year Review 1959–1978*. New York: Television Information Office, 1979.

Schein, Edgar H. *Coercive Persuasion*. New York: W. W. Norton, 1961.

Stein, Ben. *The View from Sunset Boulevard*. New York: Basic Books, 1978.

Wheeler, Michael. *Lies, Damn Lies, and Statistics: The Manipulation of Public Opinion in America.* New York: Liveright, 1976.

Wiener, Norbert. *Cybernetics or Control and Communication in the Animal and the Machine.* 2nd ed. Cambridge, Mass.: M.I.T. Press, 1961. Pp. 95 ff.

OFFICIAL REPORTS

Surgeon General's Scientific Advisory Committee on Television and Social Behavior. *Television and Social Behavior: Reports and Papers.* Technical report edited by George A. Comstock, John P. Murray, and Eli A. Rubenstein. Rockville, Md.: National Institute of Mental Health, 1972.

United States Commission on Civil Rights. *Window Dressing on the Set; Window Dressing on the Set: An Update.* Washington, D.C.: U.S. Government Printing Office, 1977, 1979.

United States Commission on Obscenity and Pornography. *The Report.* 1st ed. New York: Random House, 1971.

Part Three

CASSETTES
AND CATECHISMS

8 – *Technological Determinism and "Communications Revolutions"*

The Alteration, KINGSLEY AMIS' SPECULATIVE fiction about an alternate present that might have come about, opens in the immense Cathedral Basilica of St. George, the largest in Christendom. The occasion is the superspectacular funeral of the late English King attended in berobed splendor by most of the princes and potentates of the civilized world. Although all have come from duty, most are thrilled by the pageantry of the moment. The central jewel of the ceremony is the music and the acme of its brilliance is the near perfect voice and delivery of a boy soprano, whose talents surpass those of every singer in living memory.

"Living memory" is indeed the only touchstone of comparison for, in this speculative world imagined by Amis, electricity had never been exploited. There is no radio, no television, no recordings, not even any method to amplify sound beyond the acoustics created by architecture. Music is only experienced "live." It is either the amateurish result of one's own efforts with friends or it is a great occasion, much planned for and perhaps requiring a journey of many months, since this world has no rapid form of transportation either. This world deprived of mass media is also a world without global marketing, without atom bombs or antibiotics. It has a technology only slightly advanced beyond that of late feudalism. As a result, it is a very different world politically and culturally from the one we live in. The pope is the virtual ruler of Europe, rivaled by the equally theocratic Islam of Asia and Africa. The New World is still in a very early stage of development and the sole area where what we know as Protestantism can exist. It is a world in which organized religions and religious authorities occupy the seats of power and the founts of culture.

Amis imagines a present-day Vatican that has retained the ruthlessness of the Borgias with an added modern touch of the heartless nihilism Orwell gave his Big Brother crew. It is a moot point whether the actual twentieth century has fared any better with its genocides and advertising jingles.

In Amis' hypothesis this very different world came about because Martin Luther, instead of creating the Reformation, simply became one more pope. Without the Reformation there was no subsequent Enlightenment, no emergence of secular science and technology. A very different world.

The book thus raises again in yet another form the perennial problem of determinism. What makes things happen the way they do? Is there any one single overriding cause for things? Or do they just happen? If there is a main cause, is it impersonal, like technology, with manifold automatic but humanly unplanned effects? Or is it personal, all due to the choices of certain pivotally placed individuals, like Luther or Napoleon or Lenin or even Neville Chamberlain and Henry Kissinger?

Today many people do believe that technology is the pilot project, as it were, of destiny. They point, for instance, to the proliferation of the automobile in the last 50 years. The automobile is not just a means of transportation; it is a technology, that is, an entire social organization of tools and techniques that shapes society. The American suburbs, merchandising, our sense of community, our sexual mores, even our particular versions of human loneliness and sense of futility are all colored if not totally created by the automobile and its world of assembly lines, highway systems, garages, cruising, and back-seat romance. By extending the reach and speed of our feet, the car has changed our hearts and heads.

Others believe that technology follows rather than leads. Inventiveness and labor-saving devices are hardly necessary in a society rich in slaves. Swift long-range travel is not a goal in a culture that considers the rest of the world uninteresting and inferior. Space probes would be blasphemous for peoples who considered the heavens the exclusive province of the gods. In this view ideas are invented first; the ideas move men; then men move machines to achieve purposes the ideas have set.

A pedestrian instance of this clash of views can be found in the gun-control debate. The technological determinists say that guns kill people. The individualists or non-determinists say that people kill people. Another popular instance is in the context of mass communications. Violence and bloodshed portrayed dramatically by the mass media cause real crime and injury among the passively impressionable audience. Or, on the contrary, bad people like to blame the media for their own evil, which is reflected in the media, certainly not caused by it.

These everyday examples remind us that the determinism debate is not a sterile intellectual exercise; one's views have practical consequences for public policy because the conflict is also a moral one.

Recently, many people have come to see the advent of new communications technologies as bringing with them profound and inevitable political, social, and cultural changes; in fact, they see new technologies as forming a "communications revolution."

Unfortunately this discussion frequently takes the form of a laundry list of new devices followed by the simple assertion that they will change our lives. It is more helpful to try to see the essence of what the varieties of technologies achieve and then to review what previous communications technologies were assumed to "revolutionize" by thoughtful observers of both technology and human history.

Our thinking is clarified if we first reconceptualize the multi-faceted communications process as simply a technical procedure. We are then licensed to conceive of messages as merely material objects rather than as intangible meanings. With messages reduced to objects, communications becomes a special form of transportation, which we have long since come to think of as a technological system. Railroads, for instance, have freight yards for storage, tracks and switches for routing traffic, and terminals for transfering cargo to other modes of transport. In analogous fashion, communication systems record and store messages, address and send messages, and finally transform messages into a variety of display formats that may well differ from the form the message took in transit.

The essential technical phases of communication thus emerge as storage, traffic routing, and terminal display transformation.

Different tools, techniques, and technicians from aerospace, electronics, computer design, and less exotic fields have come together more and more efficiently in recent years to focus on the three phases of communication. There has been a spectacular advance in miniaturization of electronic components in the last few years which has greatly expanded electronic storage of information on chips and magnetic "bubbles," for instance. The videodisc, for another instance, which employs laser techniques, is basically a method of storage. One disc can store one hour of color television or 100,000 pages of print or many hours of supremely high fidelity music. Light-emitting diodes, liquid crystal display, ink-jet printers, and yet more exotic devices can display messages in almost any form; with holography, many images cannot be distinguished from the original. The microprocessor can switch and organize messages at unprecedented speeds and in extraordinarily intricate patterns. High-speed transmissions and glass wires (fiber optics) greatly expand the capacity of transmission systems so that more can be sent in less time. When these technologies are combined with space satellites the range of transmission is instantaneously worldwide.

These new technologies have already delivered high resolution color television of Jupiter across millions and millions of miles of space and are currently transforming the domestic telephone into a secretarial robot. As of this writing the *Wall*

Street Journal is edited into print on the east coast, converted and miniaturized into electronic signals, transmitted to a satellite, switched and beamed to a composing room on the west coast, where it is reconverted into print. In addition to being faster, it is a much cheaper method of getting newspapers across the country than by truck, rail, or jet.

The new communications technologies, then, reductively have three simple effects on all phases of communication. They increase storage; they speed and diversify transmission; they expand the range of display possibilities. They store, send, and show more in less space and time. The magnitudes of increase are very great, on the order of 10^4 up to 10^6 in storage capacity alone, hundreds and hundreds of thousands of times greater. Doing more with less also reduces costs at a time when prices are increasing elsewhere. The cost reduction is equally on a stupendous scale, from dollars to hundreths of a cent per unit of storage, for instance, over a period of five or six years.

For this reason, the new technologies also tend to reduce the number of competing systems. Office memos and cash, as well as newspapers, are more efficiently handled electronically. Thus, many people who condemn with Luddite doggedness the pollution and perils of modern transportation and energy technologies are delighted with the clean speed of the much invoked "information society" with its promise of the paperless office and the cashless society. Of course, Americans have long been infatuated with new devices and each generation of technological innovation brings forth a new geyser of wild hopes. James Carey has felicitously reminded us that the "electronic mythos" is but the latest version of the "technological sublime." It is such a powerful cultural force that enthusiasm for the "communications revolution" is successfully breasting the tide of distrust for big government, big business, advertising, and political propaganda.

Do these new technologies, with their breathtaking enhancement and enrichment of what is becoming—of what already is—one global system of entertainment and information, betoken a *revolution*? What has happened in the past when new improvements were in kind as well as in degree and the world seemed truly transformed?

9 – New Media Make New Worlds

ANALYSES OF PREVIOUS INNOVATIONS IN communications technology have been provided by Harold Adams Innis, an economic historian who concentrated on the Ancient Middle East; by the early Marshall McLuhan, an English professor concerned with shifts in sensibility; by Eric Havelock, a classicist fascinated by the shift from oral epic to written dialogue in ancient Greece; and by Walter Ong, a Medieval and Renaissance scholar intrigued by the influence of medium on the style of composition.

Innis, in his *Empire and Communications* and *The Bias of Communication,* saw the invention of the alphabet as a force for cultural change and social reorganization in the Ancient Middle East. From his study of the record of the cultural shifts in Egypt, Mesopotamia, Israel and other ancient cultures, he assigned a key role to the change from an oral society, where everyone was illiterate and storage was truly only in human memory, to a writing-and-reading society, with reliable records.

Oral society is local and tribal. What is remembered is put

in rhythmic form—in poetry—and organized as a story—a narrative—rather than as a theory or descriptive report. Unusual and bizarre events lodge in the mind more permanently, so legends and fables abound in oral narrative poetry. Oral societies, in large measure because of the form and content of their predominant medium, tend to be religiously organized and mythically preoccupied. The rulers of these societies are either priests themselves or they share rule with a priestly caste, which tends to be the "keeper" of the legends and myths.

The shift from ponderously inscribing hieroglyphs or ideograms on a heavy stationary medium like stone or clay to writing an alphabet on a light portable medium like papyrus enormously increased the range of activities for which exact records became possible. Empire was born, with far-reaching and clearly enforceable trade agreements. Official documents legitimizing envoys, military officers, and satraps extended the reach of central authority. The shift toward writing and records was also, Innis observed, a shift from religion and myth toward secularity and history, toward business and trade.

Eric Havelock, in his *Preface to Plato,* offers an analysis congruent to that of Innis. Havelock studied the shift from the oral epic poetry attributed to Homer and Hesiod to the written philosophical and political speculations of later Greek thinkers, notably of Plato. In doing so Havelock locates and explains Plato's seemingly strange prohibition of poetry in his ideal *Republic.*

Epic poetry had been orally composed and recited by professional bards for centuries from rote memory. It was the literature of the illiterate. The famous catalogue of ships in the *Iliad* and so many other large and small portions of the Homeric and Hesiodic *corpora* are quite clearly, for Havelock, important records and instructions for the contemporary hearers of the tales. They were being instructed while they were being entertained. Epic poetry served as a "tribal encyclopedia" with rhymed narratives that contained lessons on everything from shipbuilding to table manners. Oral tribesmen learned in a chanting singing group, often driving the lessons home with the added tempo of dancing. They were doers, not thinkers;

loyal clansmen, not solitary critics. In narrative poetry events were all explained in terms of personal agencies, mythological and polytheistic. The quarrels of the gods, their lusts and likes, their hatreds and grievances, accounted not only for the wars and sorrows, joys and loves of men, but also for the moods and tempests of nature herself.

The oral tribesman was not educated to analyze his world. He was given a set of rote formulas which, Havelock states, he tenaciously retained as "a precious horde of exemplars." More recent speculative study on the part of the brilliant and controversial Julian Jaynes of Princeton, which will be discussed in a later context, takes Havelock's analysis further—it is conceivable that ancient tribes were so far from individualism that they did not even have consciousness as we know it, building the pyramids and hearing the voices of the gods as so many directed automata. In any event, the solitary reader of the poetry of T. S. Eliot knows nothing of this tribal training function of poetry and thus, for Havelock, misapprehends Plato's political ban of it.

For Innis, communications technology fashioned the shape of society.

For Havelock, the same technology shaped the minds and hearts of its users.

Innis concentrated on the actual physical means of transmission, so that one can get the impression that oral culture is the result of the failure of alternate written technology to be adopted fully. Havelock seems to be more concerned with the "software" of ancient communication: the shape and style of oral poetry molded by the needs of people without libraries or memo pads.

In *The Gutenberg Galaxy,* an unusual, brilliant, yet exasperating collection of insights, surmise, poetic leaps, mixed with citations from a dozen disciplines and no discipline at all, Marshall McLuhan seeks to elucidate the effect of a further stage of communication technology: from writing to print to electronic media. In my opinion, the academy has too easily dismissed McLuhan because of his flashiness and his impatience with the stolid necessities of absolutely accurate historical scholarship.

McLuhan does not explain history; he exploits it in the service of his insights about the centrality of communications media. A quotable writer of enigmas, McLuhan was also much too easily adopted as a house intellectual by the popular media, most of whose harried laborers never took the time to either ponder or locate those marvelous tags he so facilely marketed: he was the media's messenger. Perhaps in large part due to this, McLuhan's later books were all too often examples of what the academy had come to despise. Nonetheless, McLuhan's orientation toward the media, his use of intellect to look at a set of puzzles previously left to hacks and accountants, and his early willingness to stoop to readable cleverness, have without a doubt been a major influence on communications study in particular and on the wider marketability of serious social criticism which "superior" scholars have not modestly shrunk from.

The central tendency of McLuhan's observations is to show that the invention of print was the ultimate triumph of the written over the spoken and that the development of audiovisual electronic media was the returning revenge of the oral over the written.

The Medieval Schoolman, who read books aloud to his students, was gradually replaced by the books. The style of writing, which for centuries aped the rhetoric, rhythms, and genre of the spoken word, began to assume its own dense, economic, "visual" forms and formats. Poetry began its long journey toward becoming the aesthetic exercise of eccentric experts. Reading became a private activity—the very antithesis of ancient tribal recitations of Homeric didactic poetry. Private judgment was the cry of the Reformation even as a written Bible, in a local language, became its weapon. Society was transformed by print which carried writing to the ends of the earth with ever greater standardization of spelling, punctuation, and usage. Innis was confirmed: the oral was local, the written led to empire.

From this perspective one can see a new reason for the accelerated separation of science from magic; science depends on accurate measurement and records whereas magic is associated with secret and sacred oral formulas, learned by heart. Business and capitalism began a global and international domination, abetted by mountains of paper marked with ink: cash, checks, bills, orders, inventories, certificates and stocks; blueprints and diaries and maps; charts navigational and charts economic. Innis was truly validated: writing was the very medium of secularity.

Such social transformations, however, were not as interesting to McLuhan as the putative inner conversion of the listener into a reader. The tribal man was "oral-aural," a joyous animal who touched and sang, dancing the steps his poetic culture traced for him. The print-oriented person was "visual," an inner being, conscious of his "psyche," which the Greeks discovered as writing grew on them. The reader is trained to use his eyes in a narrow, cruelly disciplined way, drawn by a tight string of charactered beads across a private page; he is blind to the riot of color about him and deaf to the chorus of life banned from the tomb of the library, filled with the words of the dead. The modern train commuter, isolated behind his newspaper, is shuttled between little gray rooms where he will write or read other private pages. How different, McLuhan thought, from chanting seamen heaving on their lines.

The reader-writer is linear: one word, one thought, one step at a time. He has a career; his life goes through successive stages; he has distant goals which he gradually approaches and finally achieves. The aural-oral tribesman lives in the present; he talks or sings while he works; his time is marked by the march of the days and seasons, not by the pages in a calendar.

This was the dramatically exaggerated contrast McLuhan offered to a world that was being seduced by the maturing technologies of film, television, and radio in the late fifties and early sixties. In the forties, McLuhan's *The Mechanical Bride* had anticipated the scathing elitist criticisms of Dwight Macdonald. By the sixties, he seemed to have been swept up in celebrating the triumph of neo-tribalism exalted by Norman Brown and other prophets of the Age of Aquarius. With color television developed and marketed just in time to show the horrors of the Vietnam War, with campuses inundated with war babies who were "into" film study, with the coverage of the civil rights movement by gifted technicians and artists of electronic sight and sound, McLuhan was treated as something of a prophet himself, who continually announced the death of the past: "Print is dead." "Universities are dead." Ecstatic gropers toward "Consciousness III" were "tuned in" to "McLuhanism." All these concepts are now embalmed within the quotation marks reserved for the quaint and dated.

It would be a serious error of judgment, however, to dismiss the excesses of the frenetic sixties as temporary aberrations. The seventies are not merely a replay of the fifties, with the "me generation" a slight variation on the "silent generation." The dramatic counterculture has been succeeded by the much stronger "counter" force of consumerism and while picturesque hippies have seemed to vanish, collectives, communes, and untraditional sexual arrangements have quietly multiplied. People look at more kinds of television now than they did in the sixties and the seventies have seen an unparalleled resurgence of tribalism.

Electronic media have accompanied a worldwide eruption of tribal warfare in Israel and Ireland, Nigeria and Bangladesh, North Vietnam and Cambodia. A Polish Pope and an Iranian Imam, with parallel conservatisms, have successfully defied and enthralled large corporate states with overwhelming military might standing by irrelevant and helpless. Coverage of treaties is presented in the electronic media and the print media that now are dominated by television in terms of personalities of heads of state rather than in terms of policies of governments. Astute politicians of the seventies and eighties manage media impressions rather than affairs, however pressing. Novelists and film directors, through their art, suggest the existence of entire worlds of activity through the merest hints on their respective canvases. So the politicians, in whatever walk of life, time and stage their arrivals and departures to create an impression of hurried glimpses between grinding sessions of grappling with the burdens of the earth. One suspects that after each glimpse, the grind is with the press aide and media adviser to studiously prepare the next hurried glimpse. Like the page of the novel or the set of the screen image, the glimpse itself may be all the substance that is really there. In any event, media coverage of state affairs is most often functionally indistinguishable from the global gossip that the media market so successfully from Rome to Singapore.

McLuhan's views about the return of aural-oral tribal man through electronic media with their restored orality may be in part more true today than they were in the sixties. Innis' association of print and writing with secularity and of oral society with religion may also find confirmation in much of what is happening today to the same degree.

McLuhan's error was in presuming, or at least in seeming to assume, that media replace one another. They do not. Media, like the levels of ancient cities, are layered over with successive new developments that adopt and adapt many characteristics of the previous means of communication. McLuhan himself pointed out that early films were photographed plays and early talkies were filmed plays. Radio news began as print news read aloud, and television news was originally visible reading of the radio news. With the new dominance of the electronic media, the roles are now reversed. *Time,* with its larger print, shorter sentences, proliferating color photos and dramatic graphics, strives to be a print version of a documentary. "Novelizations" are an increasing genre of prose translations of film scripts. Novels themselves are written with a cinematic viewpoint not merely because film rights are so lucrative for authors but also because the contemporary imagination is audiovisually bound.

The layering of one medium over a previous form is thus not only a matter of temporal succession and passive adjustment, it is also a situation of dynamic tensions and competition between different sensibilities and different forms of social organization.

Walter Ong takes this important developmental dimension into proper account when he calls the effect of today's electronic media *not* (as McLuhan seems to have) a simple return to aural-oral man, but rather the creation of something new-old: "secondary orality." This important difference would modify McLuhan and alter Innis.

For Innis, the written was secular and business oriented, the oral was sacred and tribal and local. Yet modern electronics are the keystone of the much touted "information society," which is serious business, indeed. Multinational conglomerates, instant global credit, teleconferencing, data processing, paperless offices with video display terminals and electronic storage in place of files, and cashless electronic transfer of money in place of primitive paper-and-ink checks, all these characteristics of modern business society which many find dehumanizing and arctically impersonal are the children of electronic aural-oral, audiovisual media. Cable services enable individuals to shop and be billed without ever leaving the sanitized security of their "home entertainment center." One can deal with an efficient and reliable machine instead of being forced to confront an unpredictable person. Trade, which has long been the spur for travel and stimulating intercultural contact from the time of the ancient caravans through Marco Polo to the Yankee clippers can now be standardized on a global scale.

Secondary orality, as a factor of social organization, has thus not merely layered over the secular rationality of print-oriented man with a simple reversion to the earlier sensibility of the tribe; it has rather presented socialized urban man with renewed opportunities for privacy, a new kind of privacy with profound political consequences.

Primary orality, in the view of Havelock, was the vehicle for absolutely untrammeled groupthink. As Plato had intuited, only the removal of oral epic poetry as dominant and its replacement with the private written word could lead to the development of the self, to critical independence, to the defiant 'I' of Luther. Media observers of the 1960's saw the great demonstrations and vast rock concerts as a return to the mindless chant and stomp of the primal group.

Secondary orality, with its vivid imagery and sound, presents the illusion of social contact without its reality. Unlike primary reality and primary orality, it is not warmly supportive; it is solipsistic. Like the isolated newspaper reader on the train, the driver tuned to his favorite news or music station is truly alone. Unlike the reader, he has the illusion of real company. Unlike the reader, he has no opportunity to exercise any judgment or critical awareness—the medium is mesmerizing. Ong has written that only the spoken, sounded word has presence. What of the taped and broadcast word? It has the illusion of presence and the reality of excluding dialogue.

Adapting Ong's view of current orality to correct the views of McLuhan and extend the scheme of Innis, I submit that we have today a form of social organization and personal sensibility that can be called "secondary tribalism." This is hardly the "global village" peopled by newly aware and alive sensitive souls for whom every bell has a perceptible, and meaningful, toll. The true village engaged the total mind and heart of aural-oral man. Secondary tribalism shares the non-critical enthusiasm of primary tribalism, but it converts the private questioning mind of the print person into an isolated observer of alien events.

Secondary tribalism has a powerful appeal for the emotions, but it is divorced from the mind, which must digest and decode the multiple demands of the "information society" with its tax forms and airline terminals. In Africa, where the colonial powers drew lines on a map (that device of written culture) which ignored the drum-filled oral-aural space of tribes, there was a cruel and heartbreaking lack of understanding between the two forms of social organization which reinforced the injustice and antagonism between exploiters and exploited. Now that the print-oriented Europeans have pulled their maps from the wall, the new nations are left with the shambles of both systems, each trying to be dominant. Through the secondary orality of the global electronic media, the earth has been "Africanized," tribalized secondarily by the conflicts, competitions, and layering of the oral-aural over the private-visual: Secondary tribalism is layered over the abstract organizational lines of the modern corporate state and of powerful multinational companies within which and beyond which it coexists in dynamic and at times threatening tension.

The outer dichotomy is mirrored in the mind, in the sensibilities of the secondary tribesman. In extreme cases it forms a terrifying schizophrenia, such as that found in the People's Temple, a group of isolates, of city dropouts seeking to discover themselves by getting lost in a South American jungle, trying to become a primary tribe at Jonestown.

Secondary tribalism is the tribalism of the Beautiful People, of the United Nations, of the Palestinian Liberation Organization and of the Irish Republican Army—all in their very disparate ways seeking wholeness through fundamentally isolating technologies. Rather than a global village, we have something like a global theater, with each person in a private box. All events, from wars to energy crises, are presented "live and in color." In such a theater, one does not debate policy; one stays or leaves; takes it or leaves it.

The Museum of Broadcasting in New York is a valuable library of audio and video tape that attempts to cover the range of broadcasting history since its beginnings. When the Museum opened in the middle seventies there was a series of introductory cocktail parties for different groups that might be supposed to have a special interest in its holdings. At the one this writer attended there were about 50 people in evidence, about a third of them connected with the Museum: the technicians, the archivists, the librarians, a generous sprinkling of professional public relations "hosts" and the distinguished director, a man who had spent a long career in broadcasting. Following a brief round of mutual introductions, the director urged the party to "turn to the monitors, please." About the Museum were a number of consoles with video monitors for the screening of videotapes. Suddenly, they all sprang to life and multiple images of the polished Alistair Cooke, that practiced electronic doorman to "classy" material, held everyone's attention as he delivered a crafted bit of Madison Avenue-ese about the Museum, followed by a series of clips from famous shows interspersed with all the cliché newsreel bits about the highlights of the twentieth century: World War I, the "Roaring Twenties," the Depression, etc.

The device of the presentational videotape was most appropriate in that it used the very facilities it was celebrating. It was also an inevitability of secondary tribalism. Here in one room were a number of people most knowledgeable about broadcasting, and the director of the Museum himself. The high point was not what any one of these living people might say to one another, nor certainly not the prospect of some sort of debate about the directions broadcasting had taken lately. It was the non-controversial, thoroughly bland and predictable, mechanical display of the apparatus. Mr. Cooke, as usual, appeared wonderfully warm and avuncularly wise, but of course he was not really there. Were any of us really there?

Perhaps the "communications revolution" has already arrived, with profound political consequences, and we have not yet noticed.

10 – *Choosing the Right Cassette*

In *That Hideous Strength,* C. S. Lewis has one of his characters surmise that as creation evolves there is a constant calving of new dichotomies; the tree of time shoots out more and more branches that fork and diverge, fork and diverge again. In the context of his story, a fairy tale that involves the return of Merlin in modern times, the division is seen in moral terms: an ever sharper difference between good and evil with less room for neutrality. Merlin in his time was a unified person but in later periods he would be forced to be either an evil sorcerer or a benign magician. Today, were his existence even remotely conceivable, he would be restricted to one of a hundred possibilities with all his magic, alas, gone: a plastic surgeon, perhaps, or a Park Avenue psychiatrist.

Leaving Lewis' context we certainly find growing divergencies in languages as they evolve. Later languages have much greater vocabularies than their ancestors for two reasons. Their users have a richer and longer experience of the world, with more things to name and talk about; they also have come to see the complex in the previously simple, to make ever more re-fined distinctions the ancients had not yet reached. No single English word, for instance, will do for the Greek *dikaiosune;* but, given a clear context, there is probably one English word for a single nuance within the primeval wholeness of the older concept.

In the languages used by the advanced industrial societies, particularly the almost universal English, functional dialects and highly developed jargons of trade have arisen. The astro-nauts spoke mostly in Engineering, in which they were fluent; on occasions of great and thrilling discoveries they switched to the Lyrical, in which they were not so fluent.

Rich as it became in associative echoes, "The Eagle has landed" is a much more precise message than Sappho's early "The moon has set and the Pleiades." In a more mysterious world, with so many of its young features as yet unclassified, each utterance carries an enchantment we can never recapture; a childlike wholeness and freshness we glimpse, perhaps, in learning the folk tales of a foreign tongue.

In the early ages of man as in the early days of life fewer choices have already been made and thus each new choice is more freshly minted, more weighted with consequence. The primitive poet chooses words heavy with whole meanings. The modern speaker chooses his idiom and then is carried along al-most automatically within that idiom. He picks a role to play and then most of his actions fit the well-worn grooves of famil-iar expectations.

In each case the modern has a far greater range of choice because he lives in a more densely varied world. But once his initial choice is made, he is on a ready-made track with little chance to improvise. The multiple world of modern man is full of standard operating procedures which have been devised step by painstaking step to reduce the terror of complexity in piloting a Concorde or in being interviewed for a job. The modern has a breathtakingly broad palette of colors, but he more than likely paints by the numbers.

The walker can control his pace and direction with almost

infinite room for improvisation, but he cannot go very far or very long and he is contained by the natural boundaries of cliff and ocean, thicket and swamp. The man on horseback can go a bit farther but with slightly less room for improvisation. The automobile, jet, and interplanetary rocket offer successive increments in power and range to the traveler who must submit at each stage to reductions in his freedom to act impulsively.

Once the astronauts were locked onto their launch pad, every minute step of the fiery path was preset by committee and computer. No individuals went to the moon; a system did. Thousands of leagues from water and soft grass, the space travelers were not free to make interesting mistakes.

So it is with the increase in power and range of communications technology. One can stumble and be brilliant by turns of chance or mood by the fireside with a few friends. One had best follow prepared notes in the lecture hall; one is taken in hand by technicians for telecasts. The primary tribal man shared a narrow set of unquestioned assumptions with his fellows from which he could say what he pleased. Electronic communicators deal with strangers, who may be rich in original ideas and most varied in background and education. But they must be reached with comprehensible messages with no chance for revision, so the range of assumptions that *all* these secondary tribesmen share may turn out to be as narrowly simplistic as the virgin worldview of primitives.

In the early days of print, as Elisabeth L. Eisenstein points out in her cautiously detailed survey, *The Printing Press as an Agent of Change,* the fears of enormously multiplied error led to a mania for exact scriptural texts in religion and an ever greater reliance on numbers and graphics over imprecise words in science. Controlling procedures intervened between the individual and the power of even the primitive press.

Modern media have brought to language the science of the standard operating procedure: a fixed and invariant formula of methods that control as rigorously as any tribal taboo. For television viewers of sports or drama there is an invariant buildup of theatrical tension every 12 minutes; broadcast edi-

torials, whimsical final news items, disaster victim interviews—
all reach the anonymous and alone mass audience with the
most common of assumed contexts.

Modern communication technologies have vastly increased
the speed and storage of signals; they deliver an enormous
freight of "information." The capacity of the human receiver,
however, cannot be enlarged proportionately. The raw unab-
sorbable information of the delivery system is thus not unlike
energy that cannot be converted into usable work; it must be
stepped down by the transformer of formulas and common expectation. The harder the hardware, so to speak, the softer the
software.

Technology has made us more free and it has made us less
free. It has lengthened our lives through medicine and short-
ened them through pollution. It has greatly increased our
range of divergent possibilities but has forced us to program
our moves and ourselves ever more rigidly.

Communications innovations have introduced this ever
greater diverging and forking effect of technology into our
thought processes and their appropriate forms of expression.

The characteristic utterance of the primary oral society was
the epic poem, the "tribal encyclopedia" chanted by tradi-
tionally motivated clans.

The characteristic utterance of the print society was the
book, a medium of private mental exchange with linear and
logical development of inner thoughts and elegant theories that
made us ponder the dreams of Descartes.

The electronic media have ushered in an age of secondary
orality and secondary tribalism—a world of divorced extremes.
The characteristic utterance of this society is the cassette: the
programmed, plug-in module of context-free thought. Cassette
communications manages to isolate what it communicates and
to keep apart and anonymous both senders and receivers of
messages. Reflecting a nation of mobile strangers without roots,
cassette communication—let us call it "cassetication"—increasingly shatters organic speech into edited bits and spots. Cassetication uses the work of artists and writers as raw material
for technicians who surgically extract the digital instructions, as

it were, from ideas so that they can be transmitted uniformly on universally adaptable tape, suitable for any kind of display system. Cassetication is the standard operating procedure for connecting isolated individuals without a context and without a foothold for critical response.

In classical rhetoric he who defined the question was usually destined to win the argument. In the mass communications era of the early and middle twentieth century, he who monopolized channels was said to control public opinion. In the age of cassetication there is neither argument to win nor public opinion to control. There is no spontaneous debate for argument. There is no public opinion in the sense of an organic, interactive, willed consensus of striving equals on any national, let alone global, scale. Publics exist only locally and fleetingly. Who gets what?

In cassetication, he who offers the final and smoothest fit of module to the system will simply manage attention. In a world of standard operating procedures, the management of attention is all that is required. Note that as the content becomes more standardized, the response becomes less human, from grudging concession to the stronger case down to bland acquiescence before the more finished product. When one chooses one's cassette, one has already chosen one's conclusion.

The secondary tribalism nurtured and serviced by cassetication carries with it a new divergence and forking.

On the one hand, there is the world of secular signals getting things done. Microprocessors and LSI-endowed computers connected by satellite and fiber optics move food, submarines, cruise missiles, natural gas, landsat photography, weather reports, sausages and champagne all over the world at great speed. They can prevent overstocking, duplication of effort, shortages, and loss of capital. They move and make money, the essence of the secular. These communication technologies form the nervous system of the so-called "knowledge society" and "manage information." This world, so proudly served by IBM, Xerox, AT&T, and other corporations, is glamorous and powerful, but we should remind ourselves that in this rhetoric a supermarket check-out clerk is a "knowledge worker" because he "processes information." It is a world without meaning, all *logos* and no *mythos,* signals without symbols save for trademarks.

On the other hand, there is the world of the "home entertainment center," worldwide tourism with computerized packaging and reservations, immediate satisfaction of curiosity with instant paperbacks, blockbuster superstars in red carpet theaters near everyone, nature interpretation centers in remote forests, instructional guides, inspirational sermons, and cautionary tales in print and on tape, on page and screen, financial advice and personal horoscopes, and, in overpowering realism, music of any type at any time summoned by fingertip. New technologies make all these recorded and thus "dead" materials seem vividly alive. Marketing economies of scale do not compel an absolute preponderance of bland midcult. Provocative themes and challenging topics, dramas and documentaries of wit and imagination are available with reasonable frequency for the metropolitan moviegoer, the viewer of public television and the listener to National Public Radio. Libraries, universities, and school systems are the beneficiaries of some stunning new methods of displaying and expositing art history, science, history, and social studies. Stories and songs can be delivered to and stored at the most remote outposts of what used to be called civilization. Oil riggers in the arctic can be entertained on a level that would have awed the most jaded Londoner of the last century. This is a world of private lives. It teems with meanings, with dreams and plans.

These diverging aspects of cassetication, the centralizing and the individuating, produce parallel constraints on all communication content. Everything must be prepared for a technical packaging and delivery system which offers no locus for moral judgment. Genuine communication requires a context but cassetication is a paradoxical invention for survival in a contextual vacuum; it thus discourages the establishment of context, of integration, of hierarchy, even as it encourages centralization of focus and outlook.

Tattooed Tears, a *cinema vérité* documentary distributed by PBS in 1979, showed the inside of a prison for young male criminals; a rough view of tough guys in a brutal place. Obscene language and menacing tones, degrading but absolutely necessary body searches for deadly weapons, blank, numb faces, dead souls and despair flooded the screen. There was one cheering note. The boys were learning skills; they were learning how to spell, how to type, how to read. They did this in a learning center. There were no teachers in evidence. There were teaching *machines*, little video- and audio-cassetted wonders which gently corrected, in Mary Poppins' tones, and earnestly congratulated each properly performed step in the carefully programmed operating procedures the machines were designed to impart. These snarling killers and maimers who continue to commit violent and obscene crimes in prison, obeyed the disembodied voice of the cassette. How can you get mad at the machine that is there to help you?

The solitary home viewer of this televised film might reflect on this perhaps unintended irony of life at a "correctional facility" as a symbol of our new age of managed and managing communication technologies. As in 23% of all American households, however, he would have no one to talk to about this idea and thus it might pass away, painlessly, to make way for the next item on the program schedule, the one constant companion available to almost every American.

Cassetication is here, embedded in the ethos of secondary tribalism. Cassetication is IBM, AT&T, CBS, and McGraw-Hill. Cassetication is a presidential press conference or a congressional hearing. Johnny Carson, Walter Cronkite, Billy Graham, The Grateful Dead, and Zubin Mehta live in cassettes. And cassetication is, for this moment, disco: tribal dancing with every beat, every strobe flash programmed by market-tested formula.

The information society rocks around the clock.

11 – *Automating Authority*

In Arthur Miller's recently revived play, *The Price*, two brothers meet in middle life, one a successful doctor, the other a police sergeant near retirement. The policeman is bitter that he did not attend medical school since, in the Depression, he felt obliged to stay home and care for his father. The doctor confronts the policeman with the immaturity of his bitterness. He had chosen the civil service security of the police because he was afraid he might not be able to hack it in medical school; his genuine love for his father served as an excellent excuse for avoiding the challenge which his brother, not without some selfishness, met and overcame. Childishly, he is now bitter, as if his own decision had not shaped his life. Adults accept responsibility for their lives. It is the price of freedom.

In previous traditional societies, where so many life decisions are culturally automatic, the burden of freedom is minimized. In modern mass-mediated society even success can be interpreted as relative failure, as failed potential, when at the touch of a button we can see the dramatized triumphs of others made to seem not so very different from ourselves. At a time when we are led to value freedom for its own sake and to see careers and life-styles as a matter of personal choice, we are absolutely naked before perceived failure. How do we avoid paying the price?

Our protection is to break life into a myriad fragments, with a professional expert in charge of each. We blame pediatricians if our children fall ill, real estate brokers if our homes are unsuitable. Leaders, before whom the buck has been alleged to stop, are most expert at exploiting specialized consultants, from "czars" to special prosecutors, as lightning rods for criticism. They have preserved the ancient practice of kings who consulted omens and soothsayers by consulting opinion polls. If a policy fails or a product proves poisonous, executives can cite polls or market research to show they were only giving the public what they were "scientifically" shown to want. Like Nixon voters, the culpable public is magically elusive. And, of course, pollsters and pundits, financial advisers and psychiatrists have elevated protective ambiguity into a refined technique that surpasses Delphi.

As of this writing, Jimmy Carter, state governors, oil companies, OPEC—all responsible parties—declare their prerogatives in deciding what is best for everyone in the alleged "energy crisis" and at the same time make it absolutely clear they had nothing to do with whatever has gone wrong. They are not unlike bankers, who have pyramided empires from extended credit and so-called "liability management," sagely citing excessive demand as the cause of inflation.

Ironically, therefore, the cultural fragmentation and technical rationality which have made the risk of failure so much more psychologically intolerable also provide the means to sidestep responsibility through specialization and delegation. Cassetication suits this purpose most admirably, because it brings back some of the comfort of primary tribalism.

How are we to understand this?

Recall the aural-oral culture of the primary tribe. Before the first millenium, B.C., the problem of personal responsibility had no ready ground to arise from.

In a brilliant and bizarrely provocative treatise, *The Origin of Consciousness in the Breakdown of the Bicameral Mind,* Julian Jaynes of Princeton presents a very strong case for ancient aural-oral man not even being conscious in the precise sense. He did not worry or debate choices. He literally heard voices when he was presented with a dilemma. What the voices said were the stored oral maxims of tribal culture, probably in poetic form. He imagined these were the "gods" inspiring him with a plan or a solution. Jaynes ambitiously speculates, with an impressive array of persuasive data, that these "voices" were stored in and produced as needed by the right hemisphere of the brain, part of which had evolved precisely for this purpose, and were what we would call today "auditory hallucinations." Jaynes surveys broad swaths of scholarship about the ancient world (in addition to brain anatomy, neurosurgery, and psychiatry) to bolster his thesis and he gives particular attention (as did Havelock) to the *Iliad,* whose gods he interprets not as mere poetic invention but as accurate portrayal of the experience of the ancient warriors, who still possessed the early "bicameral" mind.

Jaynes suggests that the invention of writing, which could localize the "voices" outside the mind (and writing can be ignored in a way spoken speech precludes), the growth of more complex societies where leaders were not personally known, nor heard, and the congress of different cultures in trade and war with different languages, and thus quite different "voices," forced the breakdown of the "bicameral" mind, with its separate compartment, as it were, for storing oral tribal wisdom. Modern schizophrenics are pathetic throwbacks to the bicameral mind.

Because of its daring and profound radicalism, Jaynes' urbanely exposited treatise may unfortunately seem, in such a brutally short summary, like the sensational crackpot theories of a Velikovsky. True or false, it is serious and profound. The bicameral hypothesis is a brilliant and apposite complement to the views and outlook of Havelock and Innis on the relationship between culture and communication.

Moreover, the bicameral hypothesis places freedom at the

heart of this relationship. Ever since the loss of the bicameral mind, we have been forced to be conscious and to that extent to be free. Once you begin to think *about* yourself, you are on the road to thinking *for* yourself. The glory of consciousness is linked to the privilege of freedom.

A parable from T. H. White's *The Once and Future King* presents this link with wit and clarity.

In White's story, Merlin the magician transforms young Wart (who will grow up to become King Arthur) into different birds and beasts, so that from this miraculous communion with the non-human he will learn both the truths of nature and the distinction of his humanity. Merlin's educational program is a sort of incarnational Aesop's Fables. It should be recalled that White wrote this book in the darkest hours of Britain's struggle with the Axis powers and in a very dark hour of his own personal life. He hated and feared fascism as a primitive throwback to brute power politics. His book was something of a lyric fairy tale to the glory of human freedom as protected by the painfully evolved British civil order.

In his tale, he captures the essential evil of fascism through the allegorical transformation of Wart into an ant.

When Wart awakens from the spell cast on him by Merlin he finds himself in a desolate area and is troubled by a constant background noise he can't quite identify. It is like a radio left on somewhere. Then he realizes that the "radio" is inside his own head; he is picking up signals from his large ant antennae. It sounds like propaganda radio, except that there is no attempt to sound interesting. The language is severely limited: there are no words for right or wrong, only "done" or "not done" which also stands for "competent/incompetent," "sane/insane." He encounters another ant and wants to ask if it is happy, what it does, and so forth, only to be faced with the utter impossibility of framing these questions with his ant vocabulary. He notices two dead ants on the road, but their cadavers are without horror or sorrow, like two pieces of furniture.

Meanwhile, the radio in his head keeps up a steady stream of directions rather like impersonal radio tower directions to aircraft, to all ants, interspersed with dreadful jingles of superpatriotism toward the nest and the queen. When a task is to be performed it is done haphazardly, without consciousness or planning. White compares the ant approach to that of a man with a teacup in one hand, a sandwich in the other, and an unlit cigarette in his mouth: if the man were an ant, he would put down the sandwich and strike a match on the teacup, then switch and strike it on the sandwich, until by sheer dumb luck, without joy or impatience, the task was done. Surrounded by these mad procedures, Wart felt the additional horror of absolutely no privacy, not even within his own mind. He was mightily relieved when Merlin whisked him back to humanity.

For Jaynes, the ant-like ancients did not know themselves and did not know freedom (or slavery). They simply could not reflect on their condition. In the transitional millenium when consciousness began to replace bicameralism, the ancients experienced a distress akin to the reverse of Wart's, as if Merlin had mistakenly pulled an ant into the teeming confusions and rich perceptions of a conscious adolescent mammal. Recourse was had to substitute voices: to oracles and soothsayers, to omens and divinations. The inner debate of consciousness was unbearable in its uncertainty and loneliness.

Whether or not one accepts the dauntingly long and deep view of Jaynes or the more modest assessment of Havelock for what Erich Fromm has called the escape from freedom, it is clear that the multiple opportunities and lack of cultural guidance that face many young Americans (and their baffled elders) have reproduced in a higher key the mental stress of bicameral breakdown and have led to a quest for the comforting simplicities of primary tribalism. From Muzak to "Newszak," the new technologies have brought to stores, restaurants, airports, elevators, and the "hold" line on the telephone, technical embodiments of White's ant colony and Jayne's theory.

Cassetication, by managing our attention so many hours of the day and night, provides us with a sort of secondary consciousness to match secondary tribalism. If humans first had to think *about* themselves in order to think *for* themselves, if consciousness was the result of the death of the "gods," of the automatic voices within our heads, then the new technologies of communications, as marketed and controlled, are bringing back voices of another sort, the cassetted companions that can reach every corner of the globe and every niche of the human mind. Secondary orality, secondary tribalism, secondary consciousness—a new iron triangle that can mean that cultural regression accompanies technical advance.

Innis saw the transformations effected by communication systems as social because communications are the vehicle and in large measure the total instrument of authority. Scholars of society, from the conservative Robert Nisbet to the radical Michael Harrington, see the current transformation as a crisis of authority too (although they would not assign to communications the central role that Innis did).

Authority is centrally involved, certainly. Jaynes sees the current successes of franchised therapies and fascistic cults as a sign of the flight to authorization. I prefer to conceptualize these phenomena as a regression toward *automatism,* which is symbiotically served by cassetication.

The automatism of cassetication exists at two levels: the level of production and the level of consumption, thus paralleling the cooperative evasion of responsibility on the parts of leaders and led.

In modern government, *automatism* is produced by the reflexive relationship cultivated between officials and their hired consultants. Pressured by lobbies, the officials turn to their advisers for a variety of scenarios and policy options. The Vietnam War, the continuing fiasco of drug traffic control, the energy crisis, land use—these are just some of the areas of challenge that have provoked tons of reports and memoranda (which the new technologies, in an electronic apotheosis of Parkinson's Law, can prodigiously store and instantly retrieve). No single adviser feels the burden of responsibility to the total real problem. He or she is comfortably in the role of piecemeal technician. The official leader, in reviewing lobby pressures and policy options, matches one from column A and one from column B on the politico-technical Chinese menu. More and more, a great deal of the options and scenarios have enjoyed considerable inputs from survey research, the computer-compiled summaries of answers to questions generated from the research about the original set of problems. Instead of borrowing the client's watch to tell him what time it is, the survey research user can check the time with legions and then return to them their own consensus.

In cassetication, original messages are taken up by scores of technicians who give them a variety of standardized treatments so that essential truth is nobody's responsibility. Technical attention is totally focused on the process, not the purpose nor content, of the communication. In turn, consumers of any given cassette pay it the compliment of uncritical half-attention, bored or dazzled by the special effects, as it were, of the message, but without concern for the import of the message itself, which by dint of repetition becomes part of the furniture of the mind.

The standard reaction to this type of observation is that it is true only of the trivial. Most of the cassetted messages observed are commercials for acne treatments. When it comes to serious matters, people pay very full attention, indeed.

This rejoinder does not hold up to any serious scrutiny.

First, commercials sell a lot more than soap. They sell political candidates and public policies, as we shall see. Second, as I have argued elsewhere, the style and attractiveness of the commercial minute, loaded with so much concentrated imaging talent, become the standard of expectation (however misguided) for all other messages.

The success of cassetication is seen in the rising position of television news as the prime source of the average person's information about the world at large and about pressing public issues. Radio news, which is second only to television and for fast-breaking crisis information surpasses television, is the epitome of cassetication. Radio uses an enormous proportion of pre-taped cassettes of actualities, edited sound from press conferences and interviews. On the all-news format, particularly, the entire day is divided into constantly recycled and gradually updated 22-minute segments, with virtually no single item exceeding 200 seconds. Both media rely increasingly on technicians to edit and shape tape into dramatic form according to formulas. "Newsrooms" are increasingly places where news is literally "made," since they are increasingly dominated by processing equipment that is geared more toward the final presentational product than toward the allegedly fact-finding and judgmental phase that should mark the beginning of the news process. Ben Bagdikian and other news critics have made this point exhaustively and our point here is not to fault the news media as such, but to focus on the domination of cassetication.

The celebrated superficialities lodged in the method of media news presentations, therefore, increasingly characterize the treatment of all facts and issues: business decisions, legislative debate, congressional and state legislative hearings and investigations. Attention to the smooth "fit" of the proper cassette, that is, to the brief and dramatic packaged presentation of any given position leaving no rough edges as possible handholds for critical questioning, dominates the erstwhile process of communications: Officials and reporters alike become spectators of various shows, from the disastrous but long-running U.S. Army press briefings in Saigon to oil company spectaculars on the true nature of the energy crisis. Increasingly boards of directors are basing more and more decisions on presentations instead of genuine information.

The ineluctable facts of blood and money caught up with both the government and the public in the Vietnamese War—after almost ten years of cassetted "factoids" to justify our presence and policies were manufactured by "communications experts" and retailed by the press, with very few exceptions. Anyone conversant with the activities of the Russian Army High Command in August of 1914, or with the Charge of the Light Brigade, knows that military and political acts of criminal cretinism are not a new invention. Vietnam was surely not the first mistaken and mismanaged war; but it was the first war where cassetication streamlined illusions for the system and made it possible for high-speed communication to be more desperately slow in real effect than dispatch riders at Waterloo. David Halberstam has rightly scolded Henry Luce and a later editor of *Time* for distorting dispatches of men in the field, following

Hearst and other magnates of the media. But of course the spirit of the age must look upon all first-hand reports as too raw, too unprocessed, too lacking in presentational fit. Expert technicians must shape material to meet the programmatic needs of the networks that carry them, as E. J. Epstein has elegantly demonstrated in *News from Nowhere*.

A moral individual is a man of his word: a solemn understanding of responsibility that goes back to tribalism. In cassetication, one cannot be a man of any word; one merely processes words, which are somehow "out there" floating in the system, produced and consumed, rather than spoken or heard. Cassetication can develop "glitches" or malfunctions, much like the navigation systems of cruise missiles, but it can never deceive, or do wrong. Missiles don't destroy countries; countries destroy countries. Politicians don't lie; advertisers don't deceive. Cassettes misfit a system.

It will be recalled that Ron Ziegler, when caught in a direct lie, did not admit to committing a deception (a lot to ask of any press secretary). He did not even admit to exaggeration or a mistake. He calmly declared that he "mis-spoke himself." A glitch in the system. Nothing personal. Cassetication is the perfect servant of the automatism that is replacing both authority and responsibility, and protects both leaders and led from the consequences of their own utterances, all the while being totally ineffectual as an interpreter of reality or as a means to shape reality to intentions, proper or not. An episode connected with Watergate, which underscored the institutional duplicity we are involved in, serves as an exemplar of this process.

In his study of the Watergate plumbers, *Agency of Fear,* E. J. Epstein gives us a glimpse of cassetication in essence.

According to Epstein's report, Nixon wished to deliver on his 1968 campaign promise to do something about crime in the streets. His staff realized, however, that the federal government has no jurisdiction over crime in the streets, which are all local law enforcement matters. But the Federal Treasury does have jurisdiction over illegal trafficking in drugs and narcotics. If drug traffic were a significant part of street crime, or even better, a notable *cause* of street crime, the connection would serve as an excellent entree for the White House to show its righteous muscle.

As readers of newspapers and viewers of television crime drama will recall, the early seventies saw a veritable epidemic of drug abuse, drug-related crime, and a bewildering number of federal initiatives to deal with the problem, from the Special Action Office for Drug Abuse Prevention to the creation of the Drug Enforcement Administration, which lives on. Whatever the measure of drug abuse in the early seventies, there is no substantial evidence that it is in any degree less now than then, although, like Soviet espionage, we hear less about it (as of this writing).

Epstein makes a very strong case for the position that a relatively constant and minor (on the national scale) problem was elevated into a national crisis for strictly political purposes. John Ingersoll, director of the then Bureau of Narcotics and Dangerous Drugs, admits that any records of numbers of addicts are based on very flimsy evidence; he believes that before 1969 the number was underestimated and after 1970 it was greatly exaggerated. Patrick Buchanan, who wrote speeches for Nixon on the subject, by a series of arbitrary multiplications of a basic reported number of 68,000 addicts in 1969, came up with 315,000 in late 1970 and with 559,000 in 1971! These imaginative and imaginary figures, designed to convince the public of the magnitude of the problem, were beginning to have the boomerang effect of creating a new public worry under Nixon's administration. Consequently, the number of addicts was reduced to 150,000 by administrative fiat. Shades of Vietnam body counts and Equity Funding's insuring of thousands of computer created non-people!

Without going into all the details (for which the reader is referred to Epstein's gripping account), it is important to outline the nihilistic procedure whereby a group of talented men manufacture concern and facts, with technical expertise and absolutely no concern for the truth of the matter.

Under Nixon's direction, John Ehrlichman assigned Egil Krogh and Jeb Magruder, the deputy director of the White House Office of Communications, to utilize television in the fight against drug abuse. Magruder, with an advertising and merchandising background, devised a standard public relations campaign for this "fight" which was packaged like Perrier. Donfeld, Krogh's assistant, suggested a special White House conference for media executives which was very detailed: all network programming v-p's, advertising agency v-p's for television; producers and production heads of 90 per cent of prime-time programming on all American television.

The conference took place. But, of course, it was not a conference at all, but rather a cassetted show. Attorney General Mitchell addressed the executives early in the morning during which a completely pre-programmed "spontaneous" message was delivered inviting all to come to the Oval Office. After the flattered and excited executives were ushered in, Nixon delivered "off-the-cuff" remarks written by Buchanan. The rest of the day was filled with tough interviews with real addicts, movies of "cold turkey," and demonstrations of dogs sniffing out hidden dope. In short, as the memo of Magruder had directed, the program was chock-full of "audio-visual and unusual presentations."

The executives were urged to bring the "reality" of the drug problem home to all Americans. They were given "information kits" on drugs that included a telephone number for official government help in answering questions that might arise in producing a television show dealing with drugs. This meeting took place in the spring of 1970 and was followed by a very similar radio conference in the fall.

Both conferences succeeded admirably. Magruder wrote that *The Name of the Game* and *Hawaii Five-O* added segments on the problem, new series were planned, and dozens of documentaries were produced." Epstein notes that *The F.B.I., Mod Squad, Marcus Welby, M.D.,* and many other shows promised narcotics features. The 1970–71, and particularly the 1971–72 through 1973–74 seasons (producers need lead time) dished out dozens of prime-time series with all the vampire stereotypes Magruder and company could have wished, long after the federal bureaucracy shifted its attention from drug fiends to the war on cancer, the newly discovered horrors of alcoholism, and swine flu.

For anyone to ask if the drug problem were even remotely as depicted by the White House conferences or by an episode of *Kojak* (each equally part of the same cassetication process) would have been an irrelevance.

Less dramatically but more pervasively, the spread of cassetication is most evident in the use of the filmed package beyond television itself. At the 1976 political conventions both parties featured slick short presentational films of their presidential candidates, which upstaged the live presence of those very candidates. Olympic sports coverage now features pretaped cassette presentations on different stars which pre-empt the tentative and unscripted live interviews. Traveling salesmen often carry cases not filled with samples of their goods but with Super-8 film systems of their product. It is significant that customers, even professional buyers, will often accord the cassetted presentation the respectful attention they withhold from living representatives. Although high costs and low budgets limit full adaptation in school systems, cassetted audiovisuals which are orchestrated into complete courses by educational consulting firms are preferred to books and teachers because they have the cachet of *Sesame Street* formats and the automatic standardization of information doled out one digestible bit at a time. These areas of cassetication touch us all.

Less familiar to the general public is the proliferation of "media services" all across the country although concentrated in Manhattan, where there are currently over 700 large and small firms that specialize in the preparation of presentations for anyone who can pay the high costs of multimedia production—as of this writing from $1,200 to $5,000 a minute. These firms are the best indicator of the cultural shift to secondary tribalism, from logical argument or trust from long association to the surface art of presentation from one set of strangers to another. The larger firms can offer a full spectrum of presentational expertise, from live musical comedy reviews to feature-length color film or videotape. As with any technical service, the media services make no judgment on the value or content of what is said. Their judgment is based solely on the end in view—usually some kind of buying or voting behavior on the part of the intended audience. An innovative conglomerate, for instance, might wish to show new welding techniques it has perfected, utilizing new materials or tools that it has exclusive rights to. The resultant film or multimedia presentation may be sent gratis to trade and vocational schools and will present the technique as effectively as it parades the conglomerate in the prominent foreground as innovative and reliable. A major business magazine might wish to increase its advertising lineage for whiskey and other spirits. Advertisers may well be treated to a show that features endorsements from well-known top executives in liquor companies. Buyers know they will please their bosses by associating them with highly successful competitors. A good media service has experts in graphic display, so that necessary figures, comparisons, and substantial facts can be presented swiftly, painlessly, and (just perhaps) in a way that leads to only one conclusion.

Many media executives wryly admit that a good presentation, from the viewpoint of slickness and dramatic punch, becomes a competitive compulsion, even when the intended message is already well understood and even when a positive decision is virtually guaranteed. This is because the absence of such a presentation might be interpreted as a lack of faith in a product or, worse, a lack of esteem and respect for assured customers. The media service can thus become something like a wedding catering service—a symbol of caring. The result is ponderous and bewildering: direct-mail specialists, for instance, have made opening and reading a letter the consequence of sophisticated human engineering. Attention is now managed professionally.

For the average person there are literally thousands of free films from companies, tourist offices, lobbying groups, and the government. The Postal Service has a film on how to mail a letter. Along with the instruction is an accompanying aura of the Post Office as bright, efficient, and deeply caring for the public, which is really (as usual) the major obstacle to proper service.

Visitors to London, New York, Boston, Vancouver and dozens of other interesting cities can now pay to see slick multimedia presentations of the actual city they are in, which presents the place with far greater vividness and drama and excitement than a sightseeing bus or a walk down the street—and the memory of which invests these simple activities with a certain glamor.

The reader no doubt can supply his own list of cassetication exposures. It would be pompous to condemn any one of these cassettes as evil or dangerous in itself. It remains prudent to assess the total cassetication process, whereby we are all schooled to hand our attention over to bland management in a willing surrender of personal critical judgment within a controlled situation where questions need not be forbidden because they are impossible to formulate. When the show is a simple matter of tourism or a bit of fun for the boys and girls at the buyers' convention, there is no harm done. But when cassetication impinges on the world where policy decisions are made, this invasion of amoral technical rationality is ominous.

Mr. Park, the Korean paymaster for corrupt congressmen, calmly told America that he was merely doing business with Congress the way any other lobbyist does, by winning good will through the pleasing contact of refreshment and entertainment. He may have gone over the line into technical bribery, but then so do many defense contractors. Media services and public relations agencies that are hired by companies, unions, and other lobbies, can be and are in fact hired by foreign governments, who have paid for the advocacy services of wives of senators and former vice-presidents. A few years ago one of the very best media services produced a multimedia spectacular for the Venezuelan government under Carlos Perez, "Toward the Great Venezuela." Naturally patriotism and hope for the country become entwined with love and gratitude toward the incumbent administration, which is, after all, the sponsor of a very long and elaborate commercial.

Is the widespread use of cassetication in politics and business, in education and entertainment, a sign of cultural regression as a result of technical advance? There comes a moment in most chess games when the density of packed potentialities on the board becomes so intense that both players tacitly collaborate in the simplification of the game by exchanging pieces, thus bringing strategic alternatives down to manageable measure. Perhaps a similar curve of development marks civilizations? There is no doubt that with the progressive revolutions in communications techniques we have followed a developmental curve from primary tribalism and rote orality to written cultures and private questioning consciousness and now on to electronic secondary tribalism with secondary consciousness. The bewildering density of the information potentialities of the electronic globe has built up a tension that has demanded the simplicity and predictability of the cassette. The comforting standard operating procedures of mental teamwork have replaced the solitary agonies and ecstasies of the private thinker.

Many have compared communications media to different languages with reference to the "grammar of film" and the "translation" of stage plays to "teleplays." The comparison is helpful at another level of analysis as well.

The lazy user of language is a passive possessor who is used by clichés. He has a standard and quasi-automatic string of phrases that loosely match grossly perceived and rather large parcels of common experience. Perception and thought are thus "low-fi," because the many nuances and complexities of any situation are eliminated to fit the stock categories of the language—much as a pocket radio reduces a symphony orchestra to a single source and a narrow range of frequencies. "You can't fight city hall," for instance, is applied to rather diverse occasions, from municipal taxes to terminal cancer.

The poet is an active exploiter of the rich density and variety of possibilities that language affords the painstaker. He uses one word at a time, chosen to match an unrepeatable particular experience acutely and minutely perceived so that auditors and readers will have their cued memories rearranged to recreate, in "hi-fi," the conveyed truth. "The water shines like tin / In the alarming light." Each word in this line of Thomas Merton's does a specific job in rearranging our common perceptions into a new and startling connection. Each tiny unit of a poem represents a fresh choice by the poet; one word does not lead on automatically to the next. The greater the creativity, the less room for automatism, the greater the freedom used, and the more responsible the author for language that bears his own unique stamp.

Moving beyond poetic diction to the larger scale of total literary genre, the same contrast between the higher fidelity of the custom-chosen creation to the lower fidelity of the cliché-dictated prevails. On the genre level, the cliché is the formula: standardized detective stories, gothic romances, musical comedies, and space operas are all examples of literary automatism. Once again, the more a writer departs from predictable formulas, the more he exercises freedom, and the more responsible he is for the result.

Cassetication falls between the micro-automatism of the cliché and the macro-automatism of the genre formula. It is the automatism appropriate to modern communications technologies, the standardized low-fidelity unit that makes the high-fidelity capacities of the technologies less intimidating.

Although Jeb Magruder's memo referred to the "unusual presentations" as a feature of the White House Conference, he was of course referring to quite standard cassettes of any well funded public relations campaign, complete with "photography opportunities" and "panel discussions." What was unusual was the wholesale and bald application of such merchandising techniques to matters of pressing public urgency (to wit, street crime, which ironically was never addressed directly because of its jursidictional inconvenience). When one racks one's brains for the dramatic apart from the substance of what should be conveyed, one comes up with dogs sniffing dope.

The White House Conference, a technical accomplishment, was the result of teamwork. It did not have the mark of any individual style. No one was totally responsible for it and certainly no one felt obliged to pledge that what was being done was the imparting of truth.

Just as each unit of the Conference was virtually an automated cassette, so the entire project was an automated response of trained technicians, who felt not the least responsible for the message, because they did not choose it—it chose them. Communication automatism, cassetication, follows the law of the large unit matching grossly perceived and large parcels of experience—low fidelity, low freedom, low responsibility, and, in this case, low politics.

Public cynicism—the hard-heart factor—is no defense against the bland persistence of cassetication. As of this writing the alleged energy crisis occupies the center stage of public attention. After Vietnam and Watergate, people are rather sceptical of government reports and industry public relations campaigns that seek to explain the problem in terms that place almost the entire burden of relief on asceticism for the masses, but greater taxes and profits for the sources of public "education" about energy. Nonetheless, as the complexities mount and as charges fly helter-skelter, something must be clung to for security, something must be believed. After 50 years of *Time* and a generation of television documentaries, simplified cassettes will conquer any attempt at a total and nuanced vision of the problem. The best sloganeers, often identical to the best paid sloganeers, will win out. Ralph Nader and Barry Commoner stand out as individuals who seem to try to speak for the public interest and who have the rare backup of organizations and research capabilities. Yet, unless they can come up with energy conferences as slick and simplified as those produced by the White House or the American Petroleum Institute, they will lose out to what we used to call the Big Lie. Commoner, for instance, is not only a brilliant analyst and expositor of intricate interrelationships; he is also willing to link his thoughts with practical politics, his most recent *The Politics of Energy* being clearly cast in an anti-Carter Administration polemic. Can his position be processed by cassetication without succumbing to the law of the large unit? If it can, he will have succeeded where other would-be apostles of truth have consistently, if unconsciously, failed.

12 – From Mechanical Christianity to Mass Culture

MICHAEL REAL, IN HIS BITING yet even-handed assessment of Billy Graham as an exploiter of the media who adapts the Gospel to suit whatever administration is in power or ideology reigns, implicitly criticizes Graham for somehow stooping to mass media promotion when he has the high calling of modern apostle. Somehow or other, modern apostles must keep aloof from the methods of secular persuaders of mass opinion. Real's indignation is not uncommon, but it is misplaced. Using cassetication and earlier P. T. Barnum methods, Oral Roberts, Graham, and dozens of other electronic preachers are not corrupting Christianity in some innovative fashion. Christianity, as an international organization aimed at an international mass of undereducated bourgeois and peasants, directed by a narrowly trained professional elite, formed a sort of proto-mass culture long before Elihu Katz was around to study the secularization of leisure, as he terms it.

The standard bemoanings of mass culture found in thinkers as diverse and divergent as Herbert Marcuse, Gabriel

Marcel, Dwight Macdonald, and Hans Magnus Enzensberger were all antedated centuries ago by the elitist criticisms of Erasmus, Thomas More, and other deplorers of what John Colet, their contemporary, called "mechanical Christianity." The history of Christianity as a mass movement is replete with all the devices of automatism that bolster authoritarianism. Early Christian apologists, with their prepared lists of standard replies to common objections to Christianity, have their modern counterparts in the invariant defensive recitatives of Moon followers. Various catechisms, with their rote question-and-answer formats, are matched today by the q-and-a scripts prepared by professional communications consultants for business executives about to undergo stockholder or government grilling.

In the end, what has done the most damage to organized churches, particularly the Roman Catholic, is not so much the intellectual questioning and doubt of enlightenment or existentialist provenance, which have so little interest for the average secondary tribesman in any event. It is the substitution of secular mass culture for previous popular Christianity, with its penchant for the quasi-magical or "mechanical," a tendency so well served today by the putatively godless. Today we have secular mass culture providing problem-solving commercial jingles, national drug abuse weeks, disco crazes, transcendental meditation weekends and other franchised methods of self-improvement, peer support groups, and a bewildering variety of profitable and not-for-profit narrow-gauge therapies. Pilgrimages, relics, rosary crusades, spiritual retreats, and the sincere but amateurish counseling of the all-purpose clergy have run into professionalized competition. Missionary Christianity, which exported these cultural automatisms to the wide world, anticipated the "global reach" of Coca-colonization and contemporary "information imperialism" of the multinational communication conglomerates. The Jesuits and Dominicans of past centuries have been replaced by the Rand Corporation and the American Enterprise Institute—pledged think tanks.

Henry Luce was fittingly the son of Yankee Protestant missionaries sent to save the pagans with the truths of *Time* about the American way of life, which he interpreted in strictly midcult-masscult terms. "Pagans," from the earliest days of Christianity, were the targets of the apostles. *"Pagus"* is the Latin term for "county, rural district" and a pagan was a country bumpkin, a local yokel, not yet attuned to the Christian message so well received in the towns and cities of late antiquity. This appellation survived to describe the entire populations of the New World and the Far East and Africa "awaiting" the coming of Christianity; they were seen as a kind of cosmic local, if that is not a contradiction in terms, awaiting the good news, the Christian message that would unite all men in one faith and one baptism.

Modern mass culture, the creature of modern mass marketing, conveys an ironically parallel notion of the world population. Locals are benighted, innocent of the knowledge and power that comes with advertising, locked in a traditional system that does not recognize the sacredness of individual choice, which is best given through money. Cash and credit are impersonal, international, and grant their possessor the power to acquire not only goods but also "information," which is seen as an essentially global reality, with a unifying force not unlike the good news of the gospel, although for wholly different reasons. Just as Max Weber saw a philosophical link between Calvinism and capitalism, today we can see a profound affinity between the sociology of popular and evangelistic Christianity and the structure and motivations of mass culture, which is the fleshly incarnation of advanced capitalism.

This affinity is dramatically focused in mass communications where it is epitomized by the mentality and methods of Christian Broadcasters. Organized into a trade association that mirrors the secular National Association of Broadcasters, complete with a code of ethics, the Christian Broadcasters are functionally indistinguishable from their models. Ben Armstrong, who has headed the organization and serves as a spokesman for electronic ministers, points with pride to the advanced technology used by missionaries.

Four American Protestant organizations broadcast continually to virtually every corner of the globe: World Radio Missionary Fellowship in Miami, which reaches all of Latin

America from Quito, Ecuador; Far East Broadcasting Company of La Mirada, California; Trans World Radio of Chatham, New Jersey; and ELWA operating from Monrovia in Liberia. Dynamic clergymen combine the credibility of Cronkite with the entrepreneurial skills of the late Sol Hurok or Lord Lew Grade. Pat Robertson, for instance, founded the Christian Broadcasting Network in the last decade. As of this writing, it consists of four television stations, six radio stations, a recording company, a program service for 3,000 cable systems, a news service, and a "university." CBN, along with other Christian operations, was one of the first to have direct "uplinks" with the Westar and Satcom satellites, bypassing leased Bell landlines and connecting them directly with 60 domestic earth stations. Robertson is also the personal host of *The 700 Club*, seen in over one million homes six days a week. And Robertson, although outstanding, is far from solitary in his splendor. Jim Bakker, another successful electronic churchman, captures their spirit perfectly: "(Television) is the greatest influence in the world today. We have a better *product* than soap or automobiles. We have eternal life." (Emphasis added) One recalls Innis' and Carey's conviction that the intrinsic bias of space-binding media like radio and television is essentially secular and militaristic. The focus of these men is hard to distinguish from that of Harold Geneen or the Chairman of Pepsico.

Both commercial traders and Christian missionaries are enthralled by the electronic potential for "outreach." Their focus is on reaching millions and millions with an identical cassetted format, using new technologies for instant "feedback," and to send out printed or electronically displayed "follow-up." Statistics on the numbers of people who "choose Christ" as a result of this outreach are the apt measure of these efforts— and they duly parallel the votes, purchases, and polled responses of market-researched target audiences everywhere. The secondary consciousness of secondary tribalism has no room nor time for debate or questioning. The cassette can only deal with prepared objections which are given standard answers. The primitive "voices" of the ancient bicameral mind (as Jaynes would have it) or the rhymed slogans of the tribal encylcopedia (as Havelock sees it) are brought back in the form of the cassette-cradled sounds and images of secondary consciousness. The potentially rebellious privacy of print-oriented man is replaced by the isolated half-attention of the individual secondary tribesman.

If this is what cassetication can do to St. Paul, St. John, St. Augustine, Kierkegaard and Barth, what would it do to Professor Commoner's nuanced understanding of the politics-energy-capitalism-ecology nexus?

Further, these modern and allegedly revolutionary changes in the communications-culture connection have greatly affected the reality of political freedom and its relation to free expression, while our ideals of freedom of speech are embedded in a prior context of communications technology.

The American First Amendment and the Anglo-Saxon incidents that preceded it, such as the century-long debate over the Licensing Act(s) of Parliament, presume that the individual is a precious source of truth as well as a locus of inalienable rights. In his argument against the first Licensing Act, *Areopagitica,* John Milton linked private conscience with public policy. To deprive an individual of his right to express himself would be to deprive the state of his contribution to the collective wisdom. It was presumed that each person could think for himself and thus might have something worthwhile to tell the rest of us. More than two centuries later, John Stuart Mill repeated Milton's arguments in *On Liberty,* which has been such a source of viewpoints and outlooks for American jurists. Mill, greatly influenced by Mrs. Taylor, a feminist of great intellect, also underscored the primary place of freedom of expression among all human freedoms, because with it one had the fundamental freedom to think and to develop one's thoughts and one's inner self. If one could not speak out, one could not think within. Without thought, the soul shriveled. For Mill, consciousness, inner awareness of the rich world, was linked with conscience, inner commitment to self-transcending values. Thought was linked to action; ideas had consequences. Such was the climate of the framing of the First Amendment and the

later invocation of that Amendment to defend individual freedom and public democracy.

Today, the individual is more often pictured as a passive
consumer: a person who needs information, a member of the
public, which has a collective right to know. This right, conceived passively, is served (as so many other needs are served)
by a specialist, a hired expert, the journalist, who is engaged to
find out what we have a right to know and to tell us, even
though he may be at risk in doing so.

There is virtually no emphasis on the individual's right and
obligation to think for himself, to judge what is happening according to his own conscience, and to speak out, to express
himself. Rather, he consumes information in handy cassetted
form and then performs a limited act (voting for a major party
figure) that reflects total acceptance or total rejection of a message of large units, conveying gross perceptions. Freedom is
taking or leaving it.

Before the advent of this political aspect of secondary tribalism, enemies of free expression were outright censors,
tyrants who simply refused to let men speak, and killed or
imprisoned those who defied their bans. The state censorship
apparatus of dozens of countries keep this dread tradition alive
today. Nevertheless, the growth of satellite broadcasting direct
to the individual possessor of a cheap "earth station," personal
recording equipment (such as the cassettes that Khomeini used
in France to speak to his Iranian followers before his own as-
cendancy to tyranny), the increased speed and storage that is
transforming the system of message distribution globally, all
these technical factors will continue to put enormous pressure
on these forms of traditional tribal—because national-
istic—forms of censorship: the direct draconianism of the primary tribe.

The new controllers censor through ownership. New systems afford immense economies of scale and demand broader
and broader application to increase profit. They encourage
global centralization and are designed for the bland software
that passes boundaries and barriers smoothly. System owners
are for the most part multinational marketing companies and

the modern corporate state, which manages markets more than it controls populations. The intrinsic bias of the system toward bland and non-provocative *information,* away from critical ideas with disruptive consequences, is in the long run a more successful censor.

Christian broadcasters who know that their messages must imitate marketing methods also know that ownership grants greater control to the message sender. Therefore they are out as a group to acquire ownership of their own stations and satellites. Armstrong sees the Christian satellite as the unexpected fulfillment of biblical prophecy (Revelation 14.6) that an Angel of the Lord will save man in the last days. The angel is a solar-powered miracle of micro-electronics in synchronous earth orbit.

Satellites can only be put in orbit by advanced technological societies. Churches and corporations with a great deal of income can buy this outreach, but they must maintain vast audiences to justify such spectacularly costly methods. The process of reaching and holding thus dominates the process of reflecting and thinking about what to reach people with. Holding attention alone becomes the goal, because attention management is the essential purpose of cassetication—minimal control over ever greater targeted markets where people are spoon-fed and obediently feed back.

The tyranny of the primary tribe has not been replaced by the simple triumph of state power over individual rights. Rather, the necessity of ownership control exerts an irresistible bias toward centralization and uniformity, burying localized independence. Modern cassetication cannot tolerate paganism, in the original sense. There is only one God, and He has booked all the time on the system.

13 – Centralization and Diversity

THE WORD "TECHNOLOGY" AS OPPOSED TO "technical" and "technique," two of its cognates, denotes not only tools and devices designed to accomplish a purpose; the added "-ology" points to an organization of tools, techniques, and technicians in one complex interlocking system, like an assembly line or a phone exchange. This is particularly true of communications technology—comtech—the essence of whose purpose is connection, distribution, organization. The high state of the art of modern comtech, the new hardware, requires the interchangeability of software that the cassetication method provides, as we have seen. It also tends toward ever greater centralization, to maximize the economies of scale of the comtech system. As a technology, comtech is highly centralized; as centralized communications, the cassetication content of comtech tends toward uniformity and homogeneity. These characteristics are desirable in any technology, but they are antipathetic to the development of culture and the climate for creative art. In this, comtech shares the vices and virtues of another highly centralized technology, agribusiness, as we have seen. It also has great affinity in this regard with the energy industries.

Energy interdependence makes a New Jersey motorist dependent on a vast network that no one person really controls, but which powerful interests can bend and manipulate for reasons that have nothing intrinsically to do with energy needs. Comtech cassetication makes a secondary tribesman dependent on a globally controlled system of information distribution that is controlled by no one person but which can be expertly exploited by marketers with no intrinsic interest in either information or truth.

As of this writing, the centralized energy system of the United States, threatened at its heart by the control of oil supplies, has filled many Americans with a feeling of helpless outrage. One cannot cook a meal, flush a toilet, buy a bottle of milk without dependence on a system of great complexity—and vulnerability. Nuclear fission is a "helluva way to boil water" but that is exactly what the system—as a mix of ownership and investment opportunities apart from its material purpose—seems to require. One thinks of the huge mechanized street sweepers belching burnt oil, unable to pass parked cars, futilely squishing and squashing down filthy urban streets, past crowds of frustrated unemployed and willing human beings, sociopolitically banned from brooms. Centralization and specialization of work have created their own peculiar Catch-22.

The rationalized centralization of comtech has made each individual thought-dependent/sensory-input-dependent on a cosmic grid just as ponderously redundant. Urban commuters hear the same dozen bulletins cycled and recycled on the way to work, yet they do not have enough immediately useful information about their own close-in environment, because there is not a sufficient market for such output. Thus, a frustrated driver might find himself drilled in a tedious litany about the surface of Nicaraguan politics, but yet not know what gas stations are open in his neighborhood. An ordinary citizen living under the irradiated plume from Three Mile Island may find himself over-informed about the public statements made by senators and state officials on the cosmic gravity and national significance of his situation, but he cannot reliably find out, for days and days, whether his life is in danger or not.

Centralized energy dependence leads to absurdly expensive (for users) methods of providing individuals with power they need and with additional power they must be "educated" to want. Comtech dependence leads to absurdly redundant and costly (in hidden charges) methods of providing individuals with some useful information and refreshing entertainment and with much more useless "information overload" and deadening trash they must be conditioned to desire. Investors and owners, on the other hand, find these systems most attractive. Energy centralization requires vast capital outlays and fuel waste whose profits are privatized and whose costs are socialized through cost pass-alongs and government loan guarantees. Comtech provides vast audiences for advertisers, legions of service subscribers, and the opportunity for media tie-ins, which are nothing else from a systems point of view than recycling distribution, with increasing profit, at no additional production cost.

In *The Politics of Energy,* Barry Commoner shows in detail how America can gradually yet practically move from fossil-fueled to solar-powered systems over a period of 50 years; with realistically feasible intermediate dependence on natural gas and methane and alcohol from renewable resources like garbage, dung, and grain crops. In the move from oil to sun there will be a shift from a few megacapacity centralized plants with huge capital requirements and high distribution costs to decentralized microsources placed exactly where they are needed: heat collectors, photovoltaic cells, windmills, and other devices of the intermediate technology that E. F. Schumacher advocated. This transition will not be without pain and inconvenience, but it is an acceptable alternative to the inefficiency, danger, terror and ultimate death resulting from blind adherence to diminishing and polluting fossil fuels or globally fatal nuclear power.

Commoner develops these ideas impressively. But even if he were wrong in his systematic understanding of energy systems, his integral critique would analogously fit the comtech system most plausibly. To presently supplement and gradually supplant much of the comtech cassetication of news, opinion, and entertainment, pumped through the system with dreary regularity and uniformity, we need (forgive the expression) windmills of the mind. Some of the new technologies—in recording methods, for instance—are ideally suited for small communities and groups, for individuals with private and questioning types of consciousness; they need to be exploited by local leaders of moral awareness, for teachers of the simple and honest truth. We need to replace phony "feedback" with genuine dialogue. These values, enduring yet fragile flowers of centuries of cultural development, cannot bloom in a mercilessly mercantile centralized system.

Oil companies are vertically integrated. They own oil in the ground; drill rigs; pipelines and supertankers; oil delivery trucks; stations and gas pumps; refineries that transform crude into hundreds of usable forms, from unleaded gasoline to plastic toy oil trucks. Some policy makers see that energy centralization and price gouging may be controllable by breaking up vertical integration, so that the free market will be operative at each level of oil production and distribution.

Comtech companies are also vertically integrated, and the new technologies that unify all communications into electronic signals for both storage and transmission make vertical integration more attractive than ever. Publishers own chains of bookstores. Networks own publishers, production companies, radio stations, research think tanks, and textbook firms. Newspapers own cable television systems; phone companies own computer systems and computer companies own satellites. Some policy makers feel that the elimination of comtech vertical integration would lead to greater diversity, and thus greater freedom among both producers and consumers of communications.

If variety and heterogeneity are desirable in culture and art, then diversity is demanded in the system that produces and distributes the artifacts of culture.

Basically, two legal strategies have been proposed to limit vertical integration in American comtech.

On the analogy with transportation, all distribution companies might be restricted to the role of "common carrier." Common carriers like busses and trains have no control at all over who is permitted to ride on them, provided each can pay the proper fare. The rates they charge can vary with circumstances, but the law forbids a rate structure that discriminates against any class of passenger (except, obviously, the poor). The telephone is mostly a common carrier, although lately it is more and more violating the strictist interpretation of that role in providing content such as Dial-a-Joke. For proponents of this strategy, the developments in both the phone company and dozens of data processing firms, most notably IBM, are not encouraging. People who make product or content, sometimes called value-added communications, are entering the distribution business in competition with Bell. At the same time Bell is entering the data processing field. Common carriers seem to be going out of style just when the critics of homogenizing comtech seem to need the concept most. Unestablished art and novel approaches to entertainment may therefore well be left on the platform, unable to beg, buy, or borrow a ticket of admission to an increasingly closed because more vertically integrated system.

Networks are in essence oligopolistic distributors of cassetication. The affiliates of the three major networks are the vast majority of all television stations. And the networks are the principal programmers of television. The wire services distribute news to broadcast and print outlets all over the world. And the wire services write, tape, and photograph most of the material that they send. The advent of new systems of distribution—satellite and cable, for the most part—have led many to believe that this sounds the deathknell to the oligopoly of the networks and will permit viable competition on a more multiple scale to the wire services. But if the same colossal conglomerates own production companies, news organizations, satellites, cable systems, data processing equipment, microwave transmission, and also manufacture receiving equipment and display systems, there will be far more vertical integration with the networks dead and buried. Accordingly, all the networks are now part of diversified conglomerates that are in all or most of the comtech activities listed. Chop off one tentacle; they will grow another. So, too, the largest oil companies are diversifying into coal, nuclear power, farming, merchandising, electrical generation.

The common carrier concept alone, therefore, would by no means guarantee non-oligopolistic sources of programming. It must be united to the second legal strategy, that of *divorcement*.

As programmers for their own distribution system, networks often produce what is programmed as well. This is universally true of network news, which is looked on as the symbolic face of the corporation that owns the network. For many people, CBS has been Walter Cronkite.

The rigid control that this self-production embodies exists to such a jealous degree that outside producers of news will only very rarely manage to get a network to buy from them. Some years ago, independent entrepreneurs peddled an exclusive video interview with Fidel Castro. No network takers. Finally, after a considerable period of time had elapsed, one of the networks got one of its own correspondents to interview Castro. Then the independent footage was bought, and intercut with shots of the network newsman interviewing Castro answering questions he had never asked and that were considerably older than the date of his visit. The common carrier concept, coupled with divorcement, would prevent this kind of practice.

As most film fans know, the thirties and forties were the apogee of the major studios in Hollywood. These major studios not only had all the big stars under contract, with internationally famous directors and writers on the payroll, they also owned chains of theaters and wholesaled their own films to their own theaters in packages of A and B films—expensive star vehicles and cheap unmemorable quickie productions. They were vertically integrated. Three decades ago the Supreme Court compelled the majors to "divorce" themselves from distribution and exhibition. Since that time the economics of the film business has made individual stars and directors independent agents, with the studios as financial backers and leasers of technical facilities. Many believe—a suit has been dragging through the courts now for the past decade enjoining the networks to get out of production—that a more widespread and radical divorcement throughout the communications industries—the entire comtech system—would increase competition and enable diversity to replace the "blandiose" programming that dominates broadcasting and other media as well. No producer could also own the means of distribution and exhibition, and all channels would be common carriers, with regulated rates.

Such American rules as divorcement may not work in the eighties, however, because comtech is multinational and conglomerated. The film business has evolved again from the independent agent stage of the late fifties and sixties. Now international sales and distribution agreements encourage the international super-blockbuster star-studded formula like *A Bridge Too Far*, which Joseph Levine presold around the world in order to bankroll the huge star cast, whose hiring, of course, guaranteed the global sales. The series, which is the trademark of an industrial imaging process, has branched out from the marketing methods of the vertically integrated television system, into the allegedly "divorced" film industry—*Jaws, The French Connection,* and other films have become formulas for sequels which are not even given different titles, all in imitation of the colossally, as they say, successful James Bond films. Large comtech conglomerates, with a multinational spread like EMI, make practical divorcement improbable. The success of longer-form television productions, from 90-minute *Columbo* to miniseries like *From Here to Eternity* (expanded from a successful film of a generation ago), as potential feature films in other countries, have further blurred the line between previously separate branches of the media. Comtech and cassetication form a hydra that no one nation is likely to dismember.

If divorcement is conducive to diversity, then the future would seem to hold less promise of diversity than the past. But perhaps diversity is a concept too little examined in itself; too easily accepted as a distinguishing mark, rather than as a necessary condition of programming excellence; too readily mistaken for the actual freedom of expression it merely facilitates.

Compared with the United States, the United Kingdom is a tight little island, with its art, politics, literature, drama concentrated in London and its two major universities and research laboratories clustered near this center. The British, perhaps because of their climate and latitude, are also avid readers of books and periodicals and love a good verbal scrap, in Parliament, at the Oxford Union, or around the soapboxes at Hyde Park. For scores of years the British public has followed running controversies with great interest, from the Bible-Evolution battle of the nineteenth century to the two-cultures, death-of-God controversies of the postwar period, and on to the more grim divisions about labor and economic policies today.

In 1946 the FCC published a report, *Public Service Responsibility of Broadcast Licensees,* which came to be known as "The Bluebook," because of its original color. This book spelled out the practical policy implications of "the public interest" invoked by the Communications Act of 12 years before. It was written for the most part by a transplanted Englishman, Charles Siepmann, who had programmed for BBC. BBC then and now thrived on controversy—one might even say that it lapsed into controversy-mongering to meet the national appetite. BBC also had a conscious policy of promoting non-English or at least non-London programming within certain limits, to display and conserve the Welsh, Scotch, and other ethnic heritages being swamped by the powerful centralizing influence of the London megalopolis. The clashing viewpoints in a variety of controversies and the varied styles of different regions as an integral part of the programming mix can be summed up under the rubric of "diversity." Diversity was also the key concept in John Stuart Mill's *On Liberty,* which most Britishly conceived civilization as a sort of gentleman's club whose chief interest was orderly debate with a view to learning more about the world; a modern version of the Greek *agora,* a marketplace of ideas. Not surprisingly, the Bluebook translated public service to mean, in essence, diversity: Diversity of competing viewpoints and diversity of regions. In America this meant that the networks would be obliged to supply their affiliates, who were the officially responsible broadcasters, with a modicum of "controversy." The local stations themselves should see to it that local affairs of their own region are adequately attended to. Later court decisions gave these policy guidelines the force of law.

Controversy, in its original British setting, had much of the marketing flavor Americans attach to newspaper "campaigns" to improve city streets with a view primarily to improving circulation. So the controversy aspect of diversity is found frequently on American television and radio, but to a degree and in a manner that mock actual debate. First, cassetication automatically insulates any presentation from criticism; second, automation relies heavily on the prerecorded. So we often find "debaters" talking blandly to the air, trusting in some technician to position them opposite a reliably "opposing view" that has also been bagged by technology. As a result, broadcast controversies have all too often become ritual interludes in the cassetication stream.

Regionalism has a special connotation in America, recalling the Western, writers of the South, Appalachian Spring, Van Wyck Brooks' New England seasons, Mark Twain's river, and Sandburg's city. In the history of American broadcasting the trend has been toward larger and larger markets, so that regionalism was antipathetic to sales and therefore an aspect of diversity that has never found favor. Country and western music, New York detectives and California policemen provide a sort of ersatz local color. But politicians who seek national office dare not sound too regional, as did Johnson and Kennedy, each of whom delivered his region for the other in a partnership distasteful to both.

Aside from the drawing power of an occasional national disaster, the coverage of which can be prolonged through the "controversy" of who was to blame (airline crashes, nuclear plant malfunctions, etc.), serious national policy dilemmas are too nuanced for successful mass marketing. Watergate, which was a circulation windfall for journalism, is a proof of this, since it was very successfully marketed as a conflict of personalities and the downfall of King Richard in four acts.

Mass marketing goes for the middle 50 per cent of the market. The other 50 per cent is roughly broken in half at two extremes of taste, political preference, etc. So any alternate programming can only at best reach one fifth to one fourth of the total market, whereas conventional programming has a chance of reaching one half of all potential listeners. From 1953 up to the seventies the percentage of TV households actually tuned in during the month of April varied from 57 to 62. Think of all the changes in technology and programming for over 25 years, yet the percentage of viewers is virtually constant. This is why the offerings of networks are so similar and why when they change with trends, they change in virtual locked step. Regional programming, by definition, would not even get one sixth of the potential market.

Both market forces and the economies of scale encouraged by the new technologies view diversity as a disaster.

One need not be confined to the commercial market, however. The American people as taxpayers and as voluntary contributors and many large and small corporations have shown themselves willing to support public broadcasting, which can be independent of the market and follow idealistic policies of serving the public.

The Carnegie Commission, whose report on broadcasting 10 years ago served as a quasi-blueprint for the current Public Broadcasting System, has recently come forward with a new report: *A Public Trust*. This new report is an authoritative source for the thinking of policy makers in public broadcasting. In this report, once again, diversity is seen as the hallmark of communications of value. Instead of seeing the audience as a central tendency of 50 per cent of the potential market, the Carnegie Commission sees the audience as a *public*.

But how does the Commission, and Public Broadcasting, conceive of the public? Is it the core of active, educated, concerned citizens, who share in a common American heritage of the protestant work ethic, the sacredness of the individual, the importance of personal responsibility and the realistic hope for greatness to be achieved by any life in a variety of ways? Is it a group of people involved in a tradition which they have received and which they hope to pass on? No, it is not so conceived. The public for *A Public Trust* is seen as a collection of constituencies, determined by age, race, income, sex, and ethnic roots. Each fragmented constituency wants its part of the pie. Public Broadcasting should therefore act, according to the report, as a sort of communications HEW, serving up something for each group. Putting this in the jargon of the trade, the report notes that ideally PBS should have a cumulative audience of 100 per cent. This means that in the course of a month every group would see at least one program intended just for it.

As the commercial broadcasters see the audience in terms of a numerically rated collection of different demographic segments, newly marrieds, "upscale gentry," urban singles, etc., based on what they are likely to want to buy, so the public broadcasters, at least in the persons of their policy advisers and higher administrators, see the public in terms of block voters. Functionally, they are identical conceptualizations. The block-voting public, it might seem, would admit of more diversity than the central tendency of the market. A look at the schedule of PBS television, however, reveals a startling parallelism to commercial broadcasting.

The way PBS in practice sees its public is in terms of the people who actively deal with it. Minority groups who seek "representation" are offered a number of programs on the local level that are about minorities and their problems, the unexamined but reasonable assumption being that programs *about* a group are also reasonably intended *for* that group to watch—a complete reversal of Mill's notion of diversity, which meant a variety of exposures to the unfamiliar for the same person, to broaden him and extend his sympathies; the present policy entrenches parochialism. But the main group served seems to be the upper middle class with some college education up to and including professional and graduate school training. The bulk of the audience would seem to be conceived as professionals and managers.

Although the *MacNeil-Lehrer Report* would seem to be the dream of the Carnegie Commission's demographic view of diversity, the style and content of the program are aimed at managers, primarily, with their viewpoints and their colleagues mostly on camera. It is perhaps just an irony that MacNeil is a Canadian, Lehrer a Texan (drawl intact) and that Charlayne Hunter-Gault is a black woman from Georgia. Thirty uninterrupted minutes of generally unscripted discussion on a single topic are a welcome relief from the slick prepackaged cassettes of *60 Minutes,* despite its admittedly higher entertainment value and production standards. But the level of discourse at the PBS production could hardly be called controversial or diverse if we were to include outlooks and philosophies as well as different topics within our notion of diversity. One gets (and the viewing audience appreciates very much) a smooth continuum of managerial-class received wisdom.

Looking at the general PBS TV schedule for 1979–1980 one sees a picture of simply a more tony range of entertainment, heavy with soap opera and murder mysteries, unstinting in its coverage of live performances from Lincoln Center to Wolf Trap with a frequent enough sortee to Boston for a concert or two. There are sports—tennis and soccer and hockey, rather than baseball or football—self-help in health, emotions, and cooking; and, finally, there are miniseries from abroad, including that staple of the commercial cassetication system, the sequel (*Poldark II*).

With the new technologies for distribution, PBS for the first time on a national scale will be a network (that much less regionalism) by broadcasting a *core schedule,* two hours of the same programming four nights a week on most of its stations. The one type of program PBS has that does not seem to be merely a higher-toned version of what is already on commercial stations is its educational documentaries such as the *NOVA* series; this would not include the *National Geographic Specials,* which have tended to fade into allegedly amusing narratives which fail to exploit the splendid graphics.

None of these remarks is meant as a condemnation of PBS nor (certainly not!) of the professional-managerial classes (of which the author is a grateful card-carrying member). The point is that apparent alternatives to the marketing-demographic cassetication/comtech system are merely less severe versions of it. The public is invariably conceived of in terms of constituent demographics whose *needs* must be served in order to get their support as consumers/contributors/political supporters. PBS in the form of New York's WNET-TV is hardly a laggard in pleasing its supporters. As of this writing it paid the highest salaries to its top executives and had the largest overall budget of any of the stations in New York, which would include the flagship stations of the networks.

In 1977 an influential bit of market research stated:

> . . . one interesting trend that has emerged could be labeled "Conspicuous Cultivation." It has established itself over the past several years and describes the desire to display familiarity with names, facts, and cultural activities as long as it requires relatively little time and effort to do so.
>
> This indicates that such persons (*sic*) will seek out radio and television news programs, interview and talk shows, where such information can be acquired quickly and readily, and is presented in an interesting and easily absorbable fashion.
>
> The main trait of cultivation is considered to be up on current events (*sic*), but there is also a strong desire to be familiar with best-selling books everybody is talking about. To be able to identify allusions to famous people—ranging from gossip to inside information and jokes—is perceived as important.
>
> We consider this trend well established and expect it to continue.

Although the source for this was NBC Corporate Planning, it could well be imagined as an integral part and guiding light for much of the programming policy of every broadcaster, including PBS, and of every aspect of American comtech.

Neither divorcement nor the common carrier concept, therefore, are likely to bring about genuine diversity. The diversity that Mill espoused and that Siepmann commended to American broadcasting was the diversity of viewpoints and philosophies. As we have seen, the new technologies have a space-binding bias against regionalism, that might have provided occasions for diversity of outlooks being shared. We have further seen that the market mentality is inimical to almost every form of diversity. As a result, diversity in its acceptable form (for PBS, for instance) seems to be merely diversity of *topic,* but always seen from the same old angles.

Let me repeat that these problems are most dramatic and pressing in broadcasting, which is a regulated industry subject to political and therefore lobbying pressures, but they are also true of all the aspects of the comtech system. The vast variety of American magazines, for instance, is a variety of topics and interests, for the most part. The methods of presentation and their attendant viewpoints are converging monolithically. More and more specialty magazines and organizational journals feel obliged to deal with the same "celebrities" and "issues" that the mass media present. How many "diverse" magazines, for instance, feel obliged to review the same books and movies? With a shorter history and a less developed tradition, the coming plethora of audiovisual cassettes are apt to have an even more narrow range of outlooks and approaches. Think of the density of visual clichés in *Star Wars* or *Close Encounters of the Third Kind,* both products of film school graduates with an enviable command of technological effects but such a narrow range of perceptions within which to exploit them.

14 – *Technology and Morality*

IN THE FIFTIES AND SIXTIES college students and social scientists often invoked the word "society" in the way scholastic philosophers invoked "nature." When specific causes and designable human agents cannot be found for any given situation or phenomenon, attribute it to society. In the early seventies, "the environment" began to displace society as the universal cause. Today, it seems to be "technology." Everything out of the speaker's control and beyond his ken is called "technology." The Greeks had a more honestly simple linguistic refuge: *ananke,* "necessity." They saw life as full of challenging beauty and excitement, but bordered inexorably by death and the inescapable human vices which ultimately asserted themselves over the admirable, but futile, efforts of warriors, lovers, poets, and statesmen. Sophocles says that indeed necessity is stern, unremittingly austere. This tragic view of life is not without nobility or reasonableness given the lessons of history.

It may seem a bit "heavy" to place so much metaphysical freight and social commentary on the more narrow and quite clear concept of "technology." Technology is the social organization of means to accomplish material ends. Primitives have a technology of spears and advanced countries have a technology of missiles with atomic warheads. Most of the time, however, when people speak of technology they have in mind high technology: the complex bureaucratic organization of sophisticated devices. The heart is not an isolated pump; it is the focal point of an entire cardiovascular system. So, too, heart transplants are not just isolated technical operations; they are events within a high technology system of health care that involves transportation, electrical power, the law, training methods, induced attitudes of mind, special languages, and reliable institutions—in short, they are enmeshed in society and its structures. The narrow meaning of "technology" thus always suggests to the modern the rather more broad meaning of "society." Both modern concepts, because of the ungraspable complexity of their referents, now stand for "stern necessity" in the minds of the man on the street and of the professional at his desk or console.

Technology cannot exist without technicians. Modern technicians are themselves extensions of the system; they have determined, narrow, and *necessary* roles. It is significant that one of the euphemisms for a professional killer, the contract "hit man," is "mechanic." Real killers have said that their job has "nothing personal" in it; when they are given a contract, the designated victim is "already dead." If one mechanic does not do the job, another will. Although we are appalled by such people, we nevertheless remain fascinated and intrigued by them. They are so familiar in so many ways.

As we saw in our discussion of determinism, there are two fundamentally different viewpoints with regard to our freedom in the context of any one particular technology—the technology of guns or the technology of broadcasting. Yet there is a note of necessity, of determinism, of inevitability, associated with technology in general, because it is seen as a process of interlocking invariant procedures, managed by technicians who themselves are controlled by programs, guidelines, or protocols which do not and dare not leave room for individual judgment.

The ordinary individual, therefore, chooses his technicians with some trepidation, hoping they will set off on a program that will do less harm than good in the long run. This abstract statement covers very mundane experiences. Buying a car is choosing a service system, a banking system, an insurance system, and a legal system; once the choice is made, the systems go inexorably forward to process your wallet, your health, your very life.

People naturally resent this dependence on technicians, as we all resent "necessity." Nevertheless, as we have seen in our discussion of leadership and social organization, there is a numbing comfort in surrendering to a routine that puts an end to agonizing decision-making (or -evading) and renders responsibility for mistakes avoidable. One therefore willingly surrenders to an increasing domain of necessity even as one resents its encroachments.

This surrender is most sensible if one needs brain surgery or air transportation. But in recent years very ordinary activities have become subject to bizarre elaboration and specialization to a point beyond parody: choosing one's reading or wine, losing weight, meeting new friends, cheering up from a fit of the blues or a disappointment, talking to one's boss or lecturing one's subordinates, running, making hamburgers or making love.

The modern tendency to seek a technological fix for everything, even as we complain about the "impersonality" of "society," reinforces the perennial human quest for authorization. In medieval times, with religion so central to life, this frailty took the form of "mechanical Christianity," so despised by Erasmus. Our current self-enslavement to high technology may be worse simply because it is so much more thorough—it completely removes human activity from the moral plane by placing it in the hands of automatic procedures, fragmenting life into a thousand and one isolated specialties. Morality must infuse the whole of life or it touches none of life; if there is no whole, no integer, there is no integrity, its meaningful cognate.

Satirists of the past savaged the bourgeois for going piously to church services on Sunday and then sinning merrily or wearily for the rest of the week. This oft-cited hypocrisy has been replaced by a constant commitment of the self for every day of the week to a trusted technician for guidance in one narrow area of life, or, for the less well-heeled, to some peer support group, like Avarists Anonymous or Lust Learners, Inc.

The inner workings of modern communications systems require technicians of great training and skill. These technologies get messages in any form from any here to any there. As with airlines and surgeons, we cannot do without them and we are most fortunate to have them. But we must resist the temptation to make of *all* of communications (as with all of travel or all of health care) merely a collectivity of elaborate fragments exclusively the domain of designated experts. Everybody must be able to use language for a broad variety of contexts and everybody must be enabled to *judge* on the truth and beauty of any communication. Communication is the only vehicle for community. It is for the transmission of a heritage of symbols and meanings; it is not merely the social organization of techniques for sending and storing signals.

Functional market research, in tune with the times, reduces communication to a mere technology and considers symbols merely for their utility as signals—means to get people to do things. In the context of selling some goods or giving simple instructions, this is often appropriate.

In the context of politics, in the task of educating the human heart, in the mission of handing on our heritage, it is both dangerous and fatuous.

———

Selective Bibliography for Part Three

8. Technological Determinism and the "Communications Revolution"

Baer, Walter S. "Telecommunications Technology in the 1980's" from Glen O. Robinson, ed., *Communications for Tomorrow: Policy Perspec-*

tives for the 1980's. Aspen Institute for Humanistic Studies. New York: Praeger, 1978.

Giedion, Siegfried. *Mechanization Takes Command: A Contribution to Anonymous History.* New York: Oxford University Press, 1948.

Carey, James W., and J. J. Quirck. "Mythos of the Electronic Revolution," Parts I, II. *The American Scholar* 39, pp. 219–41; 395–424. (Spring, Summer, 1970).

Kranzberg, Melvin, and William H. Davenport, eds. *Technology and Culture: An Anthology.* New York: New American Library, 1972.

Mesthene, Emmanuel G. *Technological Change: Its Impact on Man and Society.* Harvard Studies in Technology and Society. Cambridge, Mass.: Harvard University Press, 1970.

9. New Media Make New Worlds

Amis, Kingsley. *The Alteration.* New York: Viking Press, 1977.

Brown Norman O. *Love's Body.* New York: Random House, 1968.

Carey, James, "Harold Adams Innis and Marshall McLuhan," *The Antioch Review,* 27, pp. 5–39. (Spring, 1967).

Ellul, Jacques. *The Technological Society.* New York: Alfred A. Knopf, 1965.

Havelock, Eric A. *Preface to Plato.* Cambridge, Mass.: Belknap Press of Harvard University Press, 1963.

Innis, Harold Adams. *The Bias of Communications.* 2nd ed. Toronto: University of Toronto Press, 1964; *Empire and Communications.* Revised by Mary Q. Innis. Toronto: University of Toronto Press, 1972.

Jaynes, Julian. *The Origin of Consciousness in the Breakdown of the Bicameral Mind.* Boston: Houghton Mifflin, 1977.

Macdonald, Dwight. *Against the American Grain.* New York: Random House, 1962.

McLuhan, Herbert Marshall. *The Gutenberg Galaxy: The Making of Typographic Man.* Toronto: University of Toronto Press, 1962; *The Mechanical Bride: Folklore of Industrial Man.* New York: Vanguard Press, 1951; *Understanding Media: The Extensions of Man.* New York: McGraw-Hill, 1964.

Marx, Leo. *The Machine in the Garden: Technology and the Pastoral Ideal in America.* New York: Oxford University Press, 1964.

Noble, David F. *America by Design: Science, Technology, and the Rise of Corporate Capitalism.* New York: Alfred A. Knopf, 1977.

Ong, Walter J. *Interfaces of the World.* Ithaca, N.Y.: Cornell University Press, 1977.

10. Choosing the Right Cassette

Barfield, Owen. *Poetic Diction: A Study in Meaning*. 3rd ed. Middletown, Conn.: Wesleyan University Press, 1973; *Speaker's Meaning*. Letchworth, Hertfordshire (U.K.): Rudolf Steiner Press, 1967.

Chomsky, Noam. *Language and Mind*. Enlarged Ed. New York: Harcourt Brace Jovanovich, 1972.

Eisenstein, Elizabeth L. *The Printing Press as an Agent of Change: Communications and Cultural Transformations in Early-Modern Europe*. 2 vols. New York: Cambridge University Press, 1979.

Lewis, C. S. *That Hideous Strength*. New York: Macmillan, 1946.

Tattooed Tears. A Documentary on Life Inside the Chino Youth Training School. Filmed by Joan Churchill and Nick Broomfield. Produced by the California Youth Authority, 1978.

11. Automating Authority

Bagdikian, Ben. "Fires, Sex, and Freaks," *The New York Times Sunday Magazine*, Oct. 10, 1976, pp. 40 ff.

Commoner, Barry. *The Politics of Energy*. New York: Alfred A. Knopf, 1979.

Diamond, Edwin. *The Tin Kazoo: Television, Politics, and the News*. Cambridge, Mass.: M.I.T. Press, 1975.

Epstein, Edward J. *Agency of Fear: Opiates and Political Power in America*. New York: G. P. Putnam's Sons, 1977. Pp. 165–172; *News From Nowhere: Television and the News*. New York: Random House, 1974.

Fordham University Communication Honors Seminar. Media Services Project: Unpublished Studies by William Ahearn, et al., 1978.

Halberstam, David. *The Powers That Be*. New York: Alfred A. Knopf, 1979. Pp. 4, 71, 81–87.

Harrington, Michael. *The Twilight of Capitalism*. New York: Simon and Schuster, 1976.

Jaynes, Julian (bis). *The Origin of Consciousness in the Breakdown of the Bicameral Mind*. Boston: Houghton Mifflin, 1977.

Merton, Thomas. "Figures for an Apocalypse," *Figures for an Apocalypse*. Norfolk, Conn.: New Directions, 1947.

Miller, Arthur. *The Price*. New York: Penguin Books, 1978.

Nisbet, Robert. *Twilight of Authority*. New York: Oxford University Press, 1975.

White, Terence H. *The Once and Future King*. New York: G. P. Putnam's Sons, 1958. Pp. 121–29.

12. From Mechanical Christianity to Mass Culture

Armstrong, Ben. *The Electric Church*. New York: Thomas Nelson, 1979.

Johnson, Paul. *A History of Christianity*. New York: Atheneum, 1976. Pp. 267 ff.

Katz, Elihu, and Michael Gurevitch. *The Secularization of Leisure*. Cambridge, Mass.: Harvard University Press, 1976.

Lifton, Robert Jay. *Thought Reform and the Psychology of Totalism*. New York: W. W. Norton, 1963.

Milton, John. *Areopagitica*.

Mill, John Stuart. *On Liberty*.

Montgomery, James. "The Electric Church: Religious Broadcasting Becomes Big Business," *The Wall Street Journal*, May 19, 1978. P. 1.

Morris, James. *The Preachers*. New York: St. Martin's Press, 1973.

Marcel, Gabriel. *Man Against Mass Society*. Chicago: Regnery, 1962.

"Pat Robertson and CBN," *Broadcasting*, March 6, 1978. Pp. 56–58.

Real, Michael R. *Mass-Mediated Culture*. Englewood, N.J.: Prentice-Hall, 1977. Pp. 152–205.

Tawney, R. H. *Religion and the Rise of Capitalism*. New York: Harcourt, Brace & World, 1926.

Weber, Max. *The Protestant Ethic and the Spirit of Capitalism*. London: G. Allen & Unwin, 1930.

13. Centralization and Diversity

Branscomb, Anne W. *The First Amendment as a Shield or a Sword: An Integrated Look at Regulation of Multi-Media Ownership*. Santa Monica, Calif.: The Rand Paper Series, 1975.

The Carnegie Commission. *A Public Trust: The Report of the Carnegie Commission on the Future of Public Broadcasting*. New York: Bantam Books, 1979.

Federal Communications Commission. *Public Service Responsibility of Broadcasting Licensees*. ("The Bluebook") Washington, D.C.: U.S. Government Printing Office, 1946.

Kopkind, Andrew. "MacNeil/Lehrer's Class Act," *Columbia Journalism Review*, Sept./Oct., 1979. Pp. 31 ff.

NBC Corporate Planning. *Broadcasting: The Next Ten Years*. New York: National Broadcasting Company, 1977. Pp. 45, 46, 77.

Owens, Bruce M., Jack N. Beebe, and Willard G. Manning. *Television Economics*. Lexington, Mass.: D.C. Heath, 1974. Pp. 95–104.
United States vs. Paramount Pictures. 334 U.S. 131 (1948).

14. Technology and Morality.

Lindblom, Charles E., and David K. Cohen. *Usable Knowledge: Social Science and Social Problem Solving*. New Haven, Conn.: Yale University Press, 1979.

Bibliographical Commentary on Method

The chasm between functionalists and humanists runs long and wide through life as well as through libraries and labs. It is not the difference between humanists and scientists, for very often scientists are humanists: Freeman Dyson and Lewis Thomas spring immediately to mind as examples. Nor is it the alleged dichotomy between "chi-squares" and "green eye-shades," the somewhat burlesqued paired stereotypes of the uneducated hard-boiled editor vs. the dithering impractical fussy professor. It is primarily a difference of sensibility that has methodological consequences. Those who see quantitative measurement as the universally apt method for understanding and who construe any staged or contrived process as some kind of valid "experiment" for testing "hypotheses" and thus yielding valid "theories" are likely to be functionalists when it comes to communication research. Those who feel that any subject of study involving the free actions of human beings requires a multiplicity of methods, only some of which are patient of numeric expression, are more probably humanistic in their approach toward understanding, and understanding precisely, any given product or process of human communication and its cultural meaning.

This basic dichotomy finds affine expression in the oppositions between behaviorism and psychoanalysis, between logical positivism and existential phenomenology, between psycholinguistics and literary criticism. Almost all fields of intellectual endeavor beyond psychology, philosophy, and language study also have some similar and equally enduring dissension.

In communication research Paul Lazarsfeld has described the difference as that between "administrative" research, which is aimed at helping institutions use means of communication for any given and usually unexamined goal, and "critical" research, which passes a judgment on the cultural value of any given type or means of communication ("Administrative and Critical Communications Research," *Studies in Philosophy and Social Science*, vol. 9, 1941). Jay G. Blumler in "Purposes of Mass Communication Research: A Transatlantic Perspective," *Journalism Quarterly*, vol. 55, #2 (Summer 1978), takes up this distinction and shows that Lazarsfeld was an administrative researcher himself. A moving force in the influential Bureau of Applied Social Research at Columbia University, Lazarsfeld was a pioneer in identifying, in practice, communications research with market research, which moves easily into political-public opinion-propaganda research since America has a promotional culture that manages markets more than it governs publics. With Elihu Katz, Lazarsfeld published the immensely important *Personal Influence* (New York: Free Press, 1955) which has made "opinion leaders" pivotal figures in the planning of propaganda campaigns, commercial and political, ever since. Joseph T. Klapper's enormously influential *The Effects of Mass Communication* (Glencoe, Ill.: Free Press, 1960) was edited by Lazarsfeld and Bernard Berelson, sponsored by the Bureau, and paid for by the Columbia Broadcasting System, the ancestor of the current communications conglomerate, CBS, Inc. Corporations, political parties—and in the days of Koreagate, the Rev. Moon, and Iranian caviar diplomacy—governments and churches pay lavish amounts for this kind of research, which now uses the latest methods of measurement with computer programming and satellite transmission. Leo Bogart, long associated with both the Bureau and the communication industry, has been providing excellent summaries and surveys of such research for many years (for example, *The Age of Television*, Third Ed., New York: Ungar, 1972; *Silent Politics*, New York: Wiley-Interscience, 1972). The impressive biographic and research survey tome, *Handbook of Communication* (Chicago: Rand McNally, 1973) is a veritable tabernacle of functional-administrative research and is edited by two superstars of government-supported research, Ithiel de Sola Pool of M.I.T. and Wilbur Schramm of Stanford. A more recent, and refreshingly reflective, survey of functional research is by Sidney Kraus and Dennis Davis, *The Effects of Mass Communication Research on Political Behavior* (University Park, Pa.: Pennsylvania State University Press, 1976).

In Blumler's scheme, T. W. Adorno's "A Social Critique of Radio Music," (*Kenyon Review*, vol. 7, Spring 1945) is an early example of critical research because it tends to take a negative view of the cultural value of the *content* of mass communications (in this instance any broadcast music, whether classical or jazz) for society viewed from a broader perspective than the narrow functionalism of administrative "value-free" research. Adorno, of course, was associated with the Frankfurt School, the nickname for that German city's very different kind of Institute for Social Research: it was frankly Marxist and anticapitalist. In this country the Institute is best known as the hatchery for the ideas of Herbert Marcuse, whose *One-Dimensional Man* (Boston: Beacon Press, 1964) was strong firewater for the burgeoning protests of radical Americans, on campus and off, during the late sixties and early seventies. Recent writers of this stamp are Hans Magnus Enzensberger (*The Consciousness Industry*, New York: Seabury Press, 1974) and Claus Mueller (*The Politics of Communication*, New York: Oxford University Press, 1974). Herbert Schiller has long been almost alone in America as a political critic of the communications establishment, particularly of its intimate connection with the military and the government (*Mass Communications and American*

Empire, New York: Augustus M. Kelley, 1969; *The Mind Managers,* Boston: Beacon Press, 1973; and *Communications and Cultural Domination,* New York: International Arts and Sciences Press, 1976). English sociologist Jeremy Tunstall in his superb collection of international media data, *The Media Are American* (London: Constable, Ltd., 1977) gives sober attention to Schiller's neo-Marxist critique of "communications and empire." Stuart Ewen's critique of American advertising (*Captains of Consciousness,* New York: McGraw-Hill, 1976) although less solemn is unmistakably in the same line of country. This kind of "critical" research seems to be, for Blumler, the only alternative to the "administrative" research practiced by so many sponsored Americans. It is mostly motivated by political ideology and mostly European, although the Americans may be catching up. My own term of "humanist" would include more kinds of communication analysis and more senses of the term "critical." Economist Harold Adams Innis (*The Bias of Communications,* Second Ed., Toronto: University of Toronto Press, 1964; *Empire and Communications,* Revised by Mary Q. Innis. Toronto: University of Toronto Press, 1972) and English professor Herbert Marshall McLuhan, in his earlier period (*The Mechanical Bride: Folklore of Industrial Man,* New York: Vanguard Press, 1951; *The Gutenberg Galaxy,* Toronto: University of Toronto Press, 1962), have provided classic criticisms of communications systems which do have an animating core of value judgments but are without ideology. The connotation of sensibility associated with the term "humanist" would also tend to exclude analysts like Enzensberger and Mueller, despite their obvious antipathy toward functional administrative research. These men share with the functionalist an almost total lack of humor and irony even when they are talking about the wellsprings of both. There is a sort of Puritan fire here that condemns programs like *All in the Family* not because they are stilted, wearisomely repetitious, and conventionally mannered but because they may instill false consciousness or support the evils of the *status quo.* Like Soviet censors, they take art so seriously because they do not take it seriously enough. Dwight Macdonald, the coiner of "midcult," need take no second seat to anyone as a political activist, yet his

Against the American Grain (New York: Random House, 1962) combines artistic sensitivity with ideological and class consciousness.

A closer parallel to the functionalist/humanist distinction is sharply studied by James Carey and Albert Kreiling in "Popular Culture and Uses and Gratifications: Notes Toward an Accommodation" from *Uses of Mass Communication: Current Perspectives on Gratifications Research,* edited by the enduring Elihu Katz and Michael Gurevitch (Los Angeles; Sage Annual Review of Research, vol. 3, 1974). Carey and Kreiling call for a "cultural analysis of meanings" rather than a tabulation of structures and stimuli. For this they invoke anthropologist Clifford Geertz' exhortation for *The Interpretation of Cultures* (New York: Basic Books, 1973) where he argues that a facade of postured scientism masks the anthropologist's failure to enter into the subjective experience of the culture he studies. Interpretation requires the sensitivity of the artist and the discipline of the litterateur to express as exactly as possible the quality of specific and particular human experiences. Borrowing from philosopher Gilbert Ryle, Geertz calls the results of such appropriately humane interpretation, "thick description."

The classic "thick description" of American media culture is still Daniel Boorstin's *The Image or What Happened to the American Dream* (New York: Atheneum, 1962). Boorstin, the man who captured and coined the "pseudo-event," is an exuberant celebrator of American society and culture, specifically of the promotional and marketing aspects so distasteful to the Frankfurt School. Yet he is certainly a humanist and not a functionalist. His later contributions (*The Democratic Experience,* New York: Random House, 1973; *The Republic of Technology,* New York: Harper and Row, 1978) are even more positive about the benefits of a marketing and media culture—but they remain incisive, apposite, and shrewd analyses. Humane and urbane criticisms of specific media institutions without any broader critique of the society in which they operate are E. J. Epstein's *News From Nowhere* (New York: Random House, 1973) wholesomely honest, thorough, acute, and devoid of methodological posturing; Les Brown's snappy and incisive *Television: The Busi-*

ness Behind the Box (New York: Harcourt Brace Jovanovich, 1971) which early showed his ability to gracefully marshall legions of facts around disarmingly direct points of argument; and Edwin Diamond's *The Tin Kazoo* (Boston: M.I.T. Press, 1975) and *Good News, Bad News* (Boston; M.I.T. Press, 1979) whose breezy tone conceals a sharp and pitiless intelligence. Although the "thickness" and intellectual weight of books like these vary, they cannot be classed with the recent spate of gossip and pop sociology about the inner cut-throat competition behind the scenes at Paramount or CBS or *The New York Times* nor with dire warnings about "mass persuasion," "subliminal seduction" nor with paeans to the "global village" of the "new technology." They are examples of, rather than studies about, mass culture and media influence.

A generation ago C. P. Snow declared concern for a growing gap between what he called the two cultures. The sciences and the humanities had become divorced in the educational system and we suddenly woke up to find university professors and senior government officials who never heard of the third law of thermodynamics and to discover laboratory grinds who could not distinguish a sonnet from an epic nor much care about either. Defective as they were, the English professor who knew not entropy might nevertheless impart literary culture to his charges and the physics professor who was a stranger to Robert Herrick might nonetheless exposit the inner intricacies of subatomic order.

Today it is not so much the gap between two kinds of legitimate and useful ways of knowing that is a problem. It is the alarming absence of any educational discipline, scientific or otherwise. The American research scene is teeming with "social scientists" who never heard of Balzac or Poincaré, Euclid or Sophocles, John Dewey or Alfred North Whitehead.

It is this vasty intellectariat, counting content and indexing pornography, that has eaten so much of our taxes to study our popular culture and to pinpoint how the media "impact" populations, peer groups, and age cohorts. It is a pity that so many media critics are ignorant of the approaches of a Harold Lasswell or a Robert Park, but it is tragic that so many communications researchers know little and care less about Edmund Wilson or T. S. Eliot.

Subject Index

Author Index